KUMON MATH WORKBOOKS

Grade 4

Decimals & Fractions

P9-DBX-860

Table of Contents

KUMON

1 Addition & Subtraction Review

Date / /

Name

Score /100

1 Add.

2 points per question

(1)
```
  2 5
+ 3 4
```

(2)
```
  1 6
+ 2 7
```

(3)
```
  3 2
+ 4 8
```

(4)
```
  2 9
+ 4 5
```

(5)
```
  6 3
+ 1 8
```

(6)
```
  4 7
+ 4 9
```

(7)
```
  5 6
+ 3 4
```

(8)
```
  5 0
+ 7 0
```

(9)
```
  6 0
+ 7 4
```

(10)
```
  5 3
+ 8 2
```

(11)
```
  6 5
+ 7 8
```

(12)
```
  9 6
+ 3 7
```

(13)
```
  1 1 8
+   2 6
```

(14)
```
  2 3 4
+   5 9
```

(15)
```
  1 5 7
+   6 8
```

(16)
```
    4 2
+ 2 9 5
```

(17)
```
    6 1
+ 3 4 9
```

(18)
```
  1 2 6
+ 2 5 7
```

(19)
```
  2 5 8
+ 1 4 2
```

(20)
```
  3 0 5
+ 1 9 5
```

Subtract.

3 points per question

(1)　 78
　　 −23

(2)　 32
　　 −14

(3)　 61
　　 −45

(4)　 54
　　 −24

(5)　 73
　　 −69

(6)　 50
　　 −28

(7)　 64
　　 −27

(8)　 100
　　 − 30

(9)　 120
　　 − 50

(10)　 167
　　 − 43

(11)　 152
　　 − 42

(12)　 134
　　 − 18

(13)　 271
　　 − 42

(14)　 363
　　 − 58

(15)　 758
　　 −326

(16)　 472
　　 −154

(17)　 640
　　 −215

(18)　 329
　　 −154

(19)　 743
　　 −278

(20)　 605
　　 −149

Do you remember your addition and subtraction?

Decimals

Level ★★

Date / 3 /2011

Name ⑤

Score /100

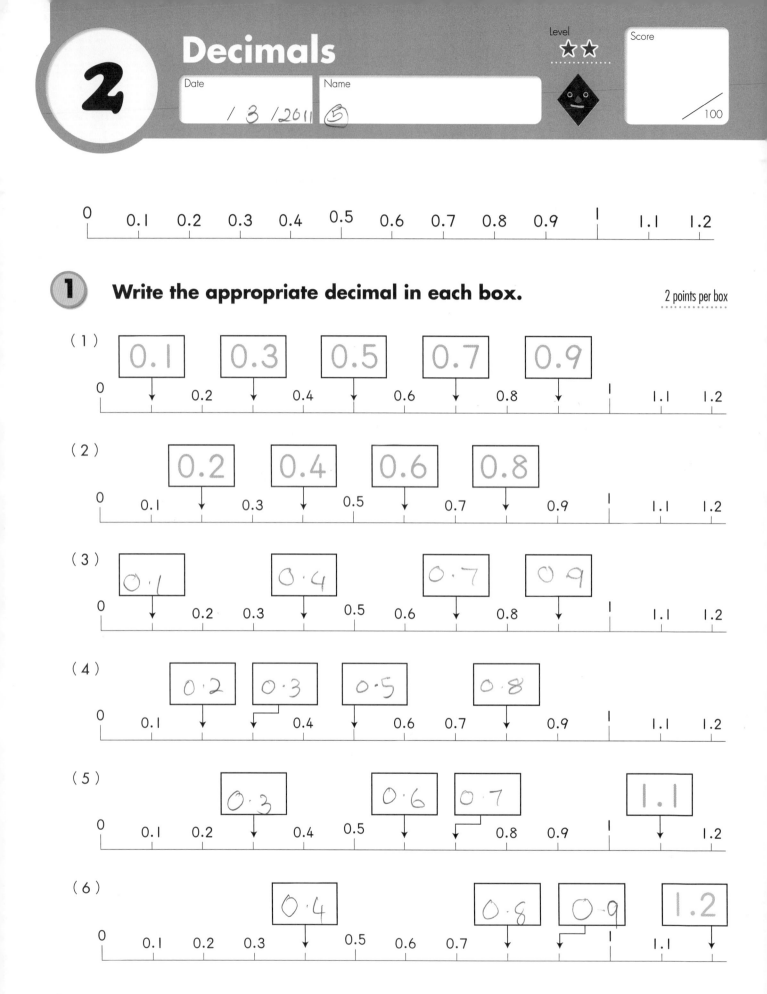

1 Write the appropriate decimal in each box.

2 points per box

(1) 0.1 0.3 0.5 0.7 0.9

(2) 0.2 0.4 0.6 0.8

(3) 0.1 0.4 0.7 0.9

(4) 0.2 0.3 0.5 0.8

(5) 0.3 0.6 0.7 1.1

(6) 0.4 0.8 0.9 1.2

© Kumon Publishing Co., Ltd.

6   3.2011

1 + .5 = 1.5

2 Write the appropriate decimal in each box.

2 points per box

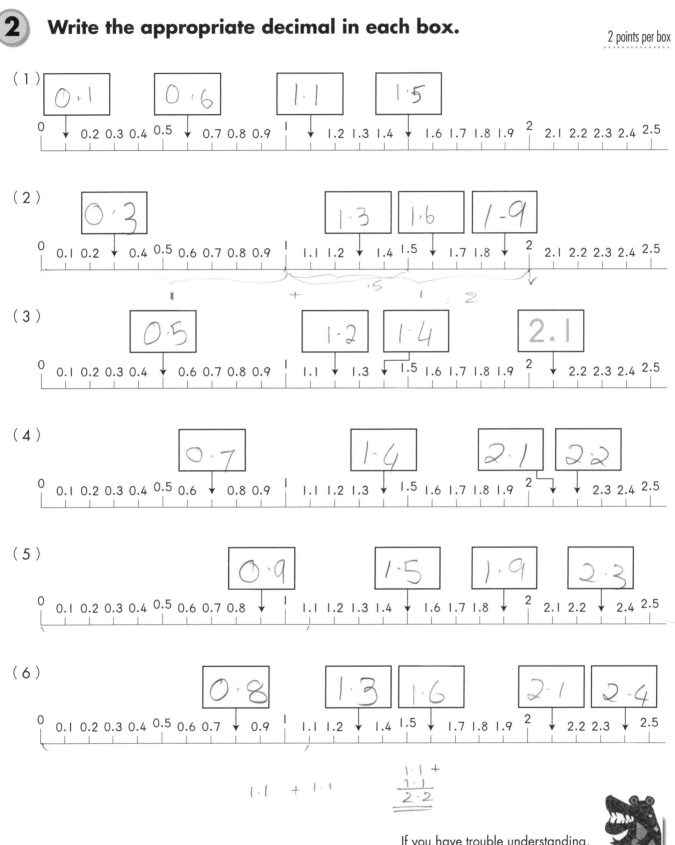

(1) 0.1   0.6   1.1   1.5

(2) 0.3   1.3   1.6   1.9

(3) 0.5   1.2   1.4   2.1

(4) 0.7   1.4   2.1   2.2

(5) 0.9   1.5   1.9   2.3

(6) 0.8   1.3   1.6   2.1   2.4

1.1 + 1.1

$$\begin{array}{r} 1.1 \\ +\ 1.1 \\ \hline 2.2 \end{array}$$

If you have trouble understanding,
try looking at the number line!

Addition of Decimals

Level ★★

Date / /

Name

Score /100

1 Add.

2 points per question

Example

$$1 + 0.2 = 1.2$$

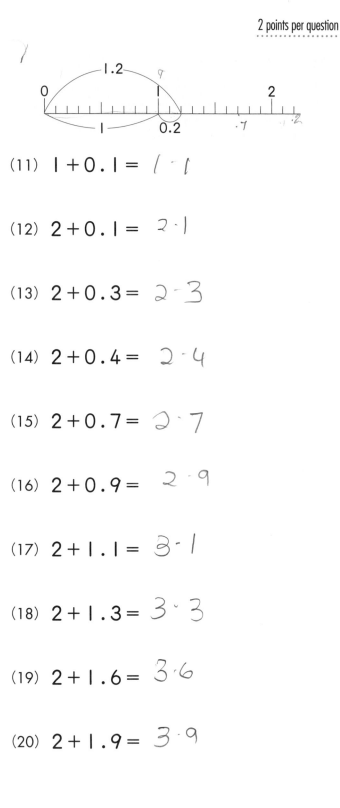

(1) $1 + 0.3 = 1.3$

(2) $1 + 0.4 = 1.4$

(3) $1 + 0.6 = 1.6$

(4) $1 + 0.7 = 1.7$

(5) $1 + 0.9 = 1.9$

(6) $1 + 1.1 = 2.1$

(7) $1 + 1.2 = 2.2$

(8) $1 + 1.3 = 2.3$

(9) $1 + 1.5 = 2.5$

(10) $1 + 1.8 = 2.8$

(11) $1 + 0.1 = 1.1$

(12) $2 + 0.1 = 2.1$

(13) $2 + 0.3 = 2.3$

(14) $2 + 0.4 = 2.4$

(15) $2 + 0.7 = 2.7$

(16) $2 + 0.9 = 2.9$

(17) $2 + 1.1 = 3.1$

(18) $2 + 1.3 = 3.3$

(19) $2 + 1.6 = 3.6$

(20) $2 + 1.9 = 3.9$

2 Add.

3 points per question

(1) 3 + 0.1 = 3·1

(2) 3 + 0.2 = 3·2

(3) 3 + 0.4 = 3·4

(4) 3 + 0.7 = 3·7

(5) 3 + 0.9 = 3·9

(6) 3 + 1.1 = 31·1

(7) 3 + 1.3 = 31·3

(8) 3 + 1.5 = 31·5

(9) 3 + 1.8 = 31·8

(10) 3 + 1.9 = 31·9

(11) 1 + 0.5 = 1·5

(12) 2 + 0.2 = 2·2

(13) 1 + 1.4 = 11·4

(14) 3 + 1.2 = 31·2

(15) 2 + 1.6 = 21·6

(16) 1 + 0.8 = 1·8

(17) 3 + 1.4 = 31·4

(18) 2 + 0.5 = 2·5

(19) 1 + 1.7 = 11·7
$$\begin{array}{r} 1\cdot1+ \\ 1\cdot0 \\ \hline 2\cdot1 \end{array}$$

(20) 3 + 1.6 = 31.6

Great work. Let's keep going!

7

Addition of Decimals

Level ★★

Score /100

Date / /

Name

1 Add.

2 points per question

Example

$$0.2 + 0.5 = 0.7$$

(1) $0.2 + 0.6 =$

(2) $0.2 + 0.7 =$

(3) $0.3 + 0.4 =$

(4) $0.3 + 0.5 =$

(5) $0.3 + 0.6 =$

(6) $0.3 + 0.7 =$

Write the answer as `1` and not `1.0.`

(7) $0.3 + 0.8 =$

(8) $0.3 + 0.9 =$

(9) $0.4 + 0.9 =$

(10) $0.5 + 0.9 =$

(11) $0.6 + 0.3 =$

(12) $0.6 + 0.4 =$

(13) $0.6 + 0.5 =$

(14) $0.7 + 0.3 =$

(15) $0.7 + 0.4 =$

(16) $0.8 + 0.4 =$

(17) $0.8 + 0.6 =$

(18) $0.8 + 0.9 =$

(19) $0.9 + 0.1 =$

(20) $0.9 + 0.4 =$

2 Add.

Example

$$1.2+0.4=1.6 \qquad 1.2+1.4=2.6$$

(1) $0.2+0.5=$

(2) $1.2+0.5=$

(3) $1.2+0.6=$

(4) $1.3+0.6=$

(5) $1.4+0.6=$

✎ Write the answer as `2' and not `2.0.'

(6) $1.4+0.7=$

(7) $1.5+0.7=$

(8) $1.6+0.7=$

(9) $1.6+0.9=$

(10) $2.6+0.9=$

(11) $1.2+0.5=$

(12) $1.2+1.5=$

(13) $1.2+1.6=$

(14) $1.2+2.6=$

(15) $1.6+1.3=$

(16) $1.6+2.3=$

(17) $2.6+3.3=$

(18) $2.4+1.2=$

(19) $2.4+2.5=$

(20) $3.4+2.3=$

Nice work!
Now let's check your answers.

Addition of Decimals

Level ★★

Date   /   /

Name

Score

/100

1 **Add.**

2 points per question

Example

$$1.6 + 2 = 3.6 \qquad 0.6 + 2 = 2.6$$

(1) $1.4 + 1 = 2.4$

(2) $1.4 + 2 =$

(3) $2.4 + 2 =$

(4) $1.7 + 1 =$

(5) $1.7 + 2 =$

(6) $1.5 + 2 =$

(7) $2.5 + 2 =$

(8) $2.8 + 1 =$

(9) $2.8 + 2 =$

(10) $3.6 + 2 =$

(11) $0.6 + 1 =$

(12) $0.7 + 1 =$

(13) $0.8 + 1 =$

(14) $0.3 + 2 =$

(15) $0.4 + 2 =$

(16) $0.6 + 2 =$

(17) $0.7 + 2 =$

(18) $0.7 + 3 =$

(19) $0.5 + 3 =$

(20) $0.9 + 3 =$

2　Add.

(1)　$1 + 0.6 =$

(2)　$3 + 1.4 =$

(3)　$0.7 + 0.5 =$

(4)　$1.2 + 0.3 =$

(5)　$2.5 + 1.3 =$

(6)　$2.8 + 2 =$

(7)　$0.4 + 3 =$

(8)　$0.6 + 0.9 =$

(9)　$1.7 + 0.3 =$

(10)　$2.3 + 3.4 =$

(11)　$0.2 + 0.7 =$

(12)　$2.6 + 0.4 =$

(13)　$2 + 1.9 =$

(14)　$0.7 + 1 =$

(15)　$0.3 + 0.8 =$

(16)　$1.4 + 2.4 =$

(17)　$0.9 + 0.1 =$

(18)　$1.2 + 3 =$

(19)　$3.6 + 1.2 =$

(20)　$0.8 + 0.6 =$

Now let's try something a bit different!

　11

6 Addition of Decimals

Level ★★

Date   /   /

Name

Score   /100

1 Add.

4 points per question

Example

$$\begin{array}{r} 2.4 \\ +1.3 \\ \hline 3.7 \end{array} \qquad \begin{array}{r} 14.2 \\ +\ 3.5 \\ \hline 17.7 \end{array}$$

When you add decimals, align the decimal points.

(1)
$$\begin{array}{r} 1.3 \\ +2.6 \\ \hline 3.9 \end{array}$$

(4)
$$\begin{array}{r} 0.4 \\ +3.5 \\ \hline 3.9 \end{array}$$

(7)
$$\begin{array}{r} 2.4 \\ +13.2 \\ \hline 15.6 \end{array}$$

(10)
$$\begin{array}{r} 0.6 \\ +5.2 \\ \hline 5.8 \end{array}$$

(2)
$$\begin{array}{r} 2.6 \\ +3.2 \\ \hline 5.8 \end{array}$$

(5)
$$\begin{array}{r} 14.3 \\ +\ 2.5 \\ \hline 16.8 \end{array}$$

(8)
$$\begin{array}{r} 0.7 \\ +12.1 \\ \hline 12.8 \end{array}$$

(11)
$$\begin{array}{r} 3.5 \\ +10.3 \\ \hline 13.8 \end{array}$$

(3)
$$\begin{array}{r} 2.6 \\ +0.2 \\ \hline 2.8 \end{array}$$

(6)
$$\begin{array}{r} 15.2 \\ +\ 0.3 \\ \hline 15.5 \end{array}$$

(9)
$$\begin{array}{r} 6.3 \\ +2.4 \\ \hline 8.7 \end{array}$$

(12)
$$\begin{array}{r} 0.4 \\ +10.4 \\ \hline 10.8 \end{array}$$

Add.

Example

```
    2.4        2.4
  + 3.8      + 3.6
  ───────    ───────
    6.2        6.0
```

(1)
```
    2.6
  + 4.2
  ───────
    6.8
```

(5)
```
    0.6
  + 2.8
  ───────
    3.4
```

(9)
```
    8.1
  + 4.9
  ───────
   13.0
```

(13)
```
    6.5
  + 7.7
  ───────
   14.2
```

(2)
```
    2.6
  + 4.7
  ───────
    7.5
```

(6)
```
    3.1
  + 4.9
  ───────
    8.0
```

(10)
```
    0.7
  + 9.3
  ───────
   10.0
```

(3)
```
    2.8
  + 0.7
  ───────
    3.5
```

(7)
```
    6.4
  + 7.2
  ───────
   13.6
```

(11)
```
    0.8
  + 4.3
  ───────
    5.1
```

(4)
```
    3.4
  + 0.6
  ───────
    4.0
```

(8)
```
    4.3
  + 6.5
  ───────
   10.8
```

(12)
```
    3.6
  + 5.6
  ───────
    9.2
```

Let's keep adding our decimals!

1 Add.

4 points per question

Example

```
   12.8        3.5         12.5
 +  3.9      +14.5       +  9
   16.7        18.0         21.5
```

(1)
```
   14.6
 +  3.1
   17.7
```

(4)
```
   12.7
 +  0.3
   13.0
```

(7)
```
    5.4
 + 12.6
   18.0
```

(10)
```
    7.9
 + 12.6
   20.5
```

(2)
```
   15.6
 +  2.7
   18.3
```

(5)
```
   13.6
 +  6.5
   20.1
```

(8)
```
    0.8
 + 12.4
   13.2
```

(11)
```
   13.4
 +  9
   22.4
```

(3)
```
   18.3
 +  4.5
   22.8
```

(6)
```
    3.5
 + 14.2
   17.7
```

(9)
```
    7.9
 + 15.2
   23.1
```

(12)
```
    7
 + 16.3
   23.3
```

2 Add.

(1) $1.6 + 3.2 = 4.8$

(2) $3.4 + 0.8 = 4.2$

(3) $5.6 + 1.4 = 7.0$

(4) $13.4 + 2.7 = 16.1$

(5) $4.2 + 12.6 = 16.8$

(6) $0.9 + 2.6 = 3.5$

(7) $4.7 + 5.5 = 10.2$

(8) $1.6 + 15.4 = 17.0$

(9) $14.6 + 8 = 94.6$

(10) $8.5 + 7.9 = 16.4$

(11) $13.2 + 0.8 = 14.0$

(12) $0.7 + 9.6 = 10.3$

(13) $10.4 + 9.8 = 20.2$

If you have difficulty solving the problems horizontally, try solving them vertically.

Have you mastered your tenths place decimals?

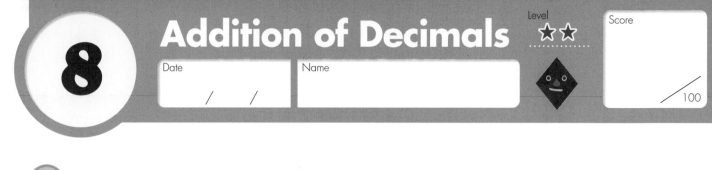

Level ★★

Date / /

Name

Score /100

1 Add.

4 points per question

Example

```
  2.36        5.73        4.76
+ 3.4       + 2.8       + 2.3
-------     -------     -------
  5.76        8.53        7.06
```

(1)
```
  2.56
+ 3.4
-------
```

(4)
```
  0.27
+ 2.6
-------
```

(7)
```
  4.35
+ 2.7
-------
```

(10)
```
  3.56
+ 4.6
-------
```

(2)
```
  4.18
+ 3.6
-------
```

(5)
```
  2.61
+ 3.8
-------
```

(8)
```
  0.73
+ 3.9
-------
```

(11)
```
  5.48
+ 0.8
-------
```

(3)
```
  3.27
+ 0.6
-------
```

(6)
```
  5.47
+ 0.9
-------
```

(9)
```
  0.83
+ 4.2
-------
```

(12)
```
  4.62
+ 3.6
-------
```

 **Add.**

(1)   5.46
    + 8.3

(5)   6.72
    + 12.3

(9)   5.44
    + 0.6

(13)   0.23
     + 0.8

(2)   5.29
    + 16.4

(6)   7.48
    + 6.9

(10)   4.37
     + 15.9

(3)   0.28
    + 12.7

(7)   7.03
    + 0.9

(11)   4.87
     + 0.6

(4)   4.36
    + 13.8

(8)   5.65
    + 7.4

(12)   0.75
     + 19.4

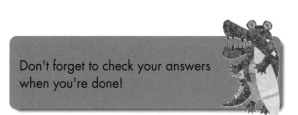

Don't forget to check your answers when you're done!

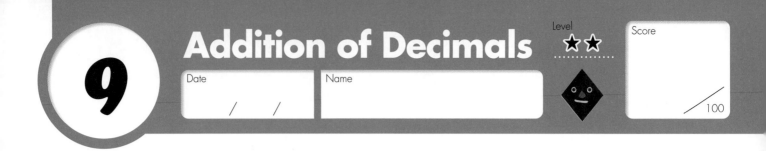

Addition of Decimals

Date / /

Name

1 Add.

4 points per question

Example

```
   2.5        4.6        2.6
 +3.16      +2.72      +3.48
  5.66       7.32       6.08
```

(1)
```
   2.4
 +3.18
```

(4)
```
   3.2
 +0.54
```

(7)
```
   2.6
 +3.47
```

(10)
```
   6.4
 +2.98
```

(2)
```
   1.6
 +4.27
```

(5)
```
   4.5
 +2.83
```

(8)
```
   4.8
 +0.25
```

(11)
```
   5.8
 +0.64
```

(3)
```
   0.3
 +3.45
```

(6)
```
   0.6
 +3.72
```

(9)
```
   0.3
 +4.72
```

(12)
```
   3.6
 +4.56
```

2 **Add.**

4 points per question

(1) 3.2
   + 8.63

(5) 13.4
   + 5.63

(9) 12.3
   + 3.84

(13) 5.2
    + 4.86

(2) 14.7
   + 8.16

(6) 6.3
   + 0.92

(10) 8.9
    + 0.16

(3) 12.5
   + 0.38

(7) 0.6
   + 9.75

(11) 14.2
    + 8.93

(4) 14.8
   + 3.64

(8) 4.7
   + 3.51

(12) 10.6
    + 0.47

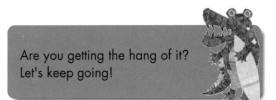

Are you getting the hang of it?
Let's keep going!

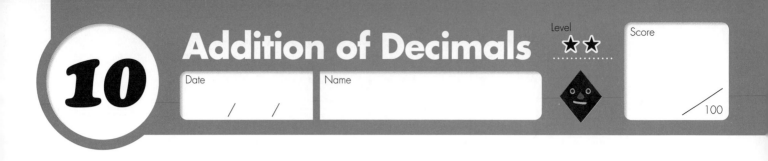

1 Add.

4 points per question

Example

```
   2.57        3.28
 +3.16       +1.52
 ─────       ─────
   5.73        4.80
```

(1)
```
   2.53
 + 3.24
```

(4)
```
   0.35
 + 5.24
```

(7)
```
   0.42
 + 2.39
```

(10)
```
   0.72
 + 3.18
```

(2)
```
   3.26
 + 4.53
```

(5)
```
   2.58
 + 3.16
```

(8)
```
   4.37
 + 1.23
```

(11)
```
   5.74
 + 1.29
```

(3)
```
   3.28
 + 0.61
```

(6)
```
   4.58
 + 0.36
```

(9)
```
   4.23
 + 0.57
```

(12)
```
   3.64
 + 5.36
```

2 Add.

4 points per question

Example

```
  2.76        4.35
+ 3.82      + 2.89
------      ------
  6.58        7.24
```

(1)
```
  4.36
+ 2.53
```

(5)
```
  2.65
+ 3.42
```

(9)
```
  0.74
+ 3.56
```

(13)
```
  3.64
+ 5.39
```

(2)
```
  3.52
+ 4.73
```

(6)
```
  3.47
+ 2.38
```

(10)
```
  4.36
+ 2.75
```

(3)
```
  3.84
+ 0.72
```

(7)
```
  3.67
+ 2.58
```

(11)
```
  6.52
+ 8.36
```

(4)
```
  0.64
+ 2.92
```

(8)
```
  4.83
+ 0.69
```

(12)
```
  4.58
+ 9.37
```

If you made a mistake, just try the problem again.
You can do it!

© Kumon Publishing Co., Ltd.   21

Addition of Decimals

Date / /

Name

Score /100

1 Add.

4 points per question

(1) 3.29
  + 2.54

(2) 4.36
  + 1.44

(3) 2.75
  + 1.63

(4) 3.28
  + 0.37

(5) 5.46
  + 2.75

(6) 4.29
  + 7.38

(7) 6.83
  + 8.25

(8) 9.08
  + 1.02

(9) 0.09
  + 0.27

(10) 0.06
  + 3.95

(11) 0.42
  + 0.76

(12) 0.96
  + 0.08

2 Add.

(1) 3.5
   + 2.73

(5) 0.64
   + 3.8

(9) 0.06
   + 0.38

(13) 0.07
    + 0.98

(2) 14.6
   + 3.92

(6) 7.84
   + 1.56

(10) 3.67
    + 6.33

(3) 3.29
   + 2.54

(7) 9.6
   + 0.72

(11) 0.85
    + 0.2

(4) 4.21
   + 0.69

(8) 7.48
   + 16.9

(12) 6.24
    + 3.8

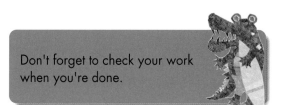

Don't forget to check your work when you're done.

Addition of Decimals

Date   /   /

Name

1 Add.

4 points per question

(1) 3.7
   + 2.9

(4) 0.52
   + 7.74

(7) 0.9
   + 5.47

(10) 0.7
   + 12.5

(2) 4.83
   + 1.3

(5) 14.2
   + 3.8

(8) 6.72
   + 1.3

(11) 8.6
    + 1.54

(3) 4.68
   + 2.16

(6) 2.03
   + 7.85

(9) 4.58
   + 7.46

(12) 9.42
    + 4.73

2 **Add.**

(1) $3.2 + 1.64 =$

(2) $4.7 + 2.8 =$

(3) $1.96 + 3.52 =$

(4) $5.06 + 0.4 =$

(5) $14.2 + 3.96 =$

(6) $2.74 + 0.16 =$

(7) $6.38 + 5.7 =$

(8) $12.9 + 3.4 =$

(9) $5.03 + 6.07 =$

(10) $0.8 + 9.5 =$

(11) $4.73 + 5.62 =$

(12) $6.92 + 5.1 =$

(13) $0.05 + 4.97 =$

If you have difficulty solving the problems horizontally, try solving them vertically.

Are you ready to try something new?

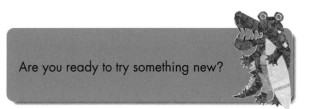

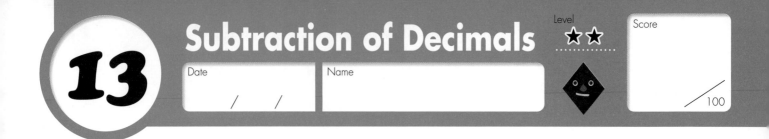

1 **Subtract.**

2 points per question

Example

$$0.7 - 0.2 = 0.5 \qquad 1.7 - 0.2 = 1.5$$

(1) $0.7 - 0.3 =$ (11) $1.7 - 0.4 =$

(2) $0.7 - 0.4 =$ (12) $1.7 - 0.6 =$

(3) $0.6 - 0.1 =$ (13) $2.7 - 0.6 =$

(4) $0.6 - 0.2 =$ (14) $2.8 - 0.6 =$

(5) $0.8 - 0.2 =$ (15) $2.8 - 0.3 =$

(6) $0.8 - 0.4 =$ (16) $1.6 - 0.3 =$

(7) $0.9 - 0.4 =$ (17) $2.6 - 0.4 =$

(8) $0.9 - 0.6 =$ (18) $3.6 - 0.5 =$

(9) $0.5 - 0.3 =$ (19) $2.9 - 0.5 =$

(10) $0.5 - 0.4 =$ (20) $3.9 - 0.7 =$

② Subtract.

Example

$$1.4 - 0.6 = 0.8 \qquad 2.4 - 0.6 = 1.8$$

(1) $1.4 - 0.3 =$

(2) $1.4 - 0.7 =$

(3) $1.4 - 0.8 =$

(4) $1.6 - 0.5 =$

(5) $1.6 - 0.6 =$

☞ Write the answer as `1`
and not `1.0.`

(6) $1.6 - 0.7 =$

(7) $1.6 - 0.9 =$

(8) $1.3 - 0.5 =$

(9) $1.3 - 0.6 =$

(10) $1.5 - 0.6 =$

(11) $2.4 - 0.3 =$

(12) $2.4 - 0.7 =$

(13) $2.4 - 0.8 =$

(14) $2.7 - 0.6 =$

(15) $2.7 - 0.7 =$

☞ Write the answer as `2`
and not `2.0.`

(16) $2.7 - 0.9 =$

(17) $3.5 - 0.3 =$

(18) $3.5 - 0.5 =$

(19) $3.5 - 0.8 =$

(20) $3.2 - 0.4 =$

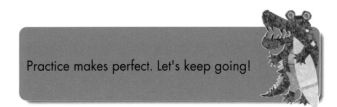

Practice makes perfect. Let's keep going!

Subtraction of Decimals

Date / /

Name

Score /100

1 Subtract.

2 points per question

Example

$$2.6 - 1 = 1.6 \qquad 1.6 - 1 = 0.6 \qquad 2.5 - 1.2 = 1.3$$

(1) $2.4 - 0.8 =$

(2) $2.4 - 0.9 =$

(3) $2.4 - 1 =$

(4) $1.4 - 1 = 0.4$

(5) $2.4 - 2 =$

(6) $2.7 - 1 =$

(7) $1.7 - 1 =$

(8) $1.3 - 1 =$

(9) $2.3 - 2 =$

(10) $3.6 - 2 =$

(11) $2.6 - 0.3 =$

(12) $2.6 - 1.3 =$

(13) $2.6 - 1.4 =$

(14) $3.8 - 1.2 =$

(15) $3.8 - 1.5 =$

(16) $3.8 - 2.5 =$

(17) $2.5 - 1.3 =$

(18) $2.5 - 2.3 =$

(19) $1.7 - 1.4 =$

(20) $3.4 - 3.1 =$

 **Subtract.**

(1) $0.8 - 0.3 =$

(2) $2.5 - 0.2 =$

(3) $1.3 - 0.7 =$

(4) $2.9 - 1.4 =$

(5) $3.2 - 1 =$

(6) $1.4 - 0.4 =$

(7) $1.6 - 1 =$

(8) $2.1 - 0.3 =$

(9) $2.5 - 1.2 =$

(10) $3.7 - 0.7 =$

(11) $2.7 - 2 =$

(12) $3.8 - 2.6 =$

(13) $2.5 - 0.5 =$

(14) $0.9 - 0.6 =$

(15) $2.3 - 0.7 =$

(16) $1.2 - 1 =$

(17) $3.6 - 0.8 =$

(18) $2.8 - 1 =$

(19) $3.7 - 2.5 =$

(20) $1.4 - 0.9 =$

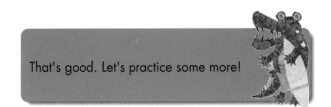

That's good. Let's practice some more!

15 Subtraction of Decimals

Date   /   /   Name

1 Subtract.

4 points per question

Example

$$\begin{array}{r} 2.5 \\ -1.2 \\ \hline 1.3 \end{array} \qquad \begin{array}{r} 13.8 \\ -1.6 \\ \hline 12.2 \end{array}$$

When you subtract decimals, align the decimal points.

(1) $\begin{array}{r} 2.7 \\ -1.2 \\ \hline 1.5 \end{array}$

(4) $\begin{array}{r} 4.7 \\ -2.6 \\ \hline 2.1 \end{array}$

(7) $\begin{array}{r} 15.8 \\ -2.4 \\ \hline 13.4 \end{array}$

(10) $\begin{array}{r} 15.6 \\ -4.4 \\ \hline 11.2 \end{array}$

(2) $\begin{array}{r} 3.6 \\ -1.4 \\ \hline 2.2 \end{array}$

(5) $\begin{array}{r} 14.5 \\ -2.3 \\ \hline 12.2 \end{array}$

(8) $\begin{array}{r} 12.9 \\ -2.7 \\ \hline 10.2 \end{array}$

(11) $\begin{array}{r} 5.9 \\ -0.2 \\ \hline 5.7 \end{array}$

(3) $\begin{array}{r} 3.6 \\ -0.4 \\ \hline 3.2 \end{array}$

(6) $\begin{array}{r} 14.7 \\ -0.3 \\ \hline 14.4 \end{array}$

(9) $\begin{array}{r} 8.4 \\ -3.1 \\ \hline 5.3 \end{array}$

(12) $\begin{array}{r} 17.7 \\ -5.6 \\ \hline 12.1 \end{array}$

2 Subtract.

Example

```
   2.5          7.3
 - 1.7        - 4.3
 ─────        ─────
   0.8          3.0
```

(1)
```
   2.6
 - 1.5
 ─────
   1.1
```

(2)
```
   2.6
 - 1.6
 ─────
   1.0
```

(3)
```
   2.6
 - 1.8
 ─────
   0.8
```

(4)
```
   2.6
 - 0.8
 ─────
   1.8
```

(5)
```
   3.2
 - 0.8
 ─────
   2.4
```

(6)
```
   3.4
 - 1.6
 ─────
   1.8
```

(7)
```
   4.7
 - 2.7
 ─────
   2.0
```

(8)
```
   5.2
 - 2.3
 ─────
   2.9
```

(9)
```
   6.3
 - 5.9
 ─────
   0.4
```

(10)
```
   5.1
 - 0.5
 ─────
   4.6
```

(11)
```
   4.3
 - 0.3
 ─────
   4.0
```

(12)
```
   9.3
 - 6.4
 ─────
   2.9
```

(13)
```
   2.4
 - 0.6
 ─────
   1.8
```

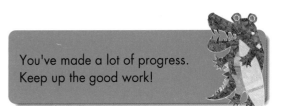

You've made a lot of progress.
Keep up the good work!

Subtraction of Decimals

Date   /   /

Name

Score

/100

1 Subtract.

4 points per question

Example

$$
\begin{array}{r}
14.6 \\
- \ \ 1.8 \\
\hline
12.8
\end{array}
\qquad
\begin{array}{r}
15.3 \\
- \ \ 2.3 \\
\hline
13.0
\end{array}
\qquad
\begin{array}{r}
13.2 \\
- \ \ 6 \\
\hline
7.2
\end{array}
$$

(1)
$$
\begin{array}{r}
14.7 \\
- \ \ 2.5 \\
\hline
\end{array}
$$

(4)
$$
\begin{array}{r}
16.3 \\
- \ \ 2.3 \\
\hline
\end{array}
$$

(7)
$$
\begin{array}{r}
16.7 \\
- \ \ 6.2 \\
\hline
\end{array}
$$

(10)
$$
\begin{array}{r}
13.4 \\
- \ \ 5.9 \\
\hline
\end{array}
$$

(2)
$$
\begin{array}{r}
14.7 \\
- \ \ 2.8 \\
\hline
\end{array}
$$

(5)
$$
\begin{array}{r}
11.5 \\
- \ \ 0.7 \\
\hline
\end{array}
$$

(8)
$$
\begin{array}{r}
14.3 \\
- \ \ 8.6 \\
\hline
\end{array}
$$

(11)
$$
\begin{array}{r}
10.6 \\
- \ \ 4.8 \\
\hline
\end{array}
$$

(3)
$$
\begin{array}{r}
15.2 \\
- \ \ 3.4 \\
\hline
\end{array}
$$

(6)
$$
\begin{array}{r}
12.4 \\
- \ \ 2.8 \\
\hline
\end{array}
$$

(9)
$$
\begin{array}{r}
15.4 \\
- \ \ 3.6 \\
\hline
\end{array}
$$

(12)
$$
\begin{array}{r}
12.5 \\
- \ \ 9 \\
\hline
\end{array}
$$

② Subtract.

(1) $4.3 - 2.7 =$

(2) $5.2 - 1.9 =$

(3) $8.6 - 3.4 =$

(4) $3.1 - 0.3 =$

(5) $15.3 - 0.6 =$

(6) $12.9 - 3.2 =$

(7) $6.4 - 5.8 =$

(8) $10.3 - 0.5 =$

(9) $8.2 - 5.2 =$

(10) $15.6 - 8.2 =$

(11) $5.6 - 3.8 =$

(12) $14.4 - 8 =$

(13) $13.6 - 3.9 =$

If you have difficulty solving the problems horizontally, try solving them vertically.

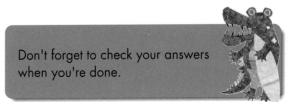

Don't forget to check your answers when you're done.

Subtraction of Decimals

Level ★★

Date / /

Name

Score /100

1 Subtract.

4 points per question

Example

```
   4.85          5.47
 − 2.3         − 1.8
 ──────        ──────
   2.55          3.67
```

(1)
```
   6.74
 − 2.3
 ──────
```

(4)
```
   4.93
 − 0.2
 ──────
```

(7)
```
   6.24
 − 1.6
 ──────
```

(10)
```
   4.26
 − 2.9
 ──────
```

(2)
```
   3.68
 − 1.5
 ──────
```

(5)
```
   5.25
 − 3.2
 ──────
```

(8)
```
   2.35
 − 0.8
 ──────
```

(11)
```
   2.41
 − 0.6
 ──────
```

(3)
```
   3.62
 − 0.5
 ──────
```

(6)
```
   7.18
 − 4.5
 ──────
```

(9)
```
   3.47
 − 0.4
 ──────
```

(12)
```
   5.03
 − 0.4
 ──────
```

Subtract.

(1) 6.25
   − 3.4

(5) 1.05
   − 0.4

(9) 3.25
   − 2.6

(13) 1.03
    − 0.2

(2) 5.25
   − 3.2

(6) 7.63
   − 2.4

(10) 4.06
    − 3.9

(3) 6.32
   − 5.7

(7) 4.38
   − 1.3

(11) 1.82
    − 0.8

(4) 5.04
   − 2.7

(8) 2.47
   − 0.7

(12) 4.05
    − 0.6

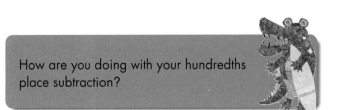

How are you doing with your hundredths place subtraction?

18

Subtraction of Decimals

Level ★★

....

Date / /

Name

Score

/100

1 Subtract.

4 points per question
....

Example

$$\begin{array}{r} 5.46 \\ -1.28 \\ \hline 4.18 \end{array} \qquad \begin{array}{r} 7.56 \\ -2.86 \\ \hline 4.70 \end{array}$$

(1)
$$\begin{array}{r} 5.76 \\ -2.34 \\ \hline \end{array}$$

(4)
$$\begin{array}{r} 2.68 \\ -0.41 \\ \hline \end{array}$$

(7)
$$\begin{array}{r} 7.84 \\ -3.29 \\ \hline \end{array}$$

(10)
$$\begin{array}{r} 5.24 \\ -3.84 \\ \hline \end{array}$$

(2)
$$\begin{array}{r} 3.87 \\ -1.63 \\ \hline \end{array}$$

(5)
$$\begin{array}{r} 5.72 \\ -2.38 \\ \hline \end{array}$$

(8)
$$\begin{array}{r} 3.52 \\ -0.15 \\ \hline \end{array}$$

(11)
$$\begin{array}{r} 3.19 \\ -0.45 \\ \hline \end{array}$$

(3)
$$\begin{array}{r} 3.97 \\ -0.53 \\ \hline \end{array}$$

(6)
$$\begin{array}{r} 6.43 \\ -2.13 \\ \hline \end{array}$$

(9)
$$\begin{array}{r} 5.38 \\ -1.72 \\ \hline \end{array}$$

(12)
$$\begin{array}{r} 1.56 \\ -0.76 \\ \hline \end{array}$$

2 Subtract.

Example

```
  4.25
- 1.49
------
  2.76
```

(1)
```
  3.27
- 1.43
```

(2)
```
  5.24
- 1.64
```

(3)
```
  4.32
- 1.15
```

(4)
```
  6.25
- 2.78
```

(5)
```
  2.36
- 0.59
```

(6)
```
  4.16
- 2.58
```

(7)
```
  3.02
- 0.64
```

(8)
```
  5.42
- 4.56
```

(9)
```
  2.83
- 0.36
```

(10)
```
  0.23
- 0.07
```

(11)
```
  6.45
- 3.92
```

(12)
```
  7.26
- 3.46
```

(13)
```
  5.04
- 0.08
```

You're doing really well!

37

Subtraction of Decimals

Level ★★

Date   /   /

Name

Score   /100

1 Subtract.

4 points per question

Example

```
  2.3          5.4
-1.16        -1.65
-----        -----
 1.14         3.75
```

(1) 2.52
   - 0.16

(4) 4.8
   - 3.25

(7) 6.2
   - 1.63

(10) 7.2
    - 1.06

(2) 2.5
   - 0.16

(5) 5.42
   - 2.78

(8) 4.5
   - 0.72

(11) 1.4
    - 0.39

(3) 3.7
   - 1.34

(6) 5.4
   - 2.78

(9) 3.2
   - 0.43

(12) 1.7
    - 0.85

Subtract.

(1)
```
   3.6
 - 2.47
```

(5)
```
   2.51
 - 0.73
```

(9)
```
   4.24
 - 3.54
```

(13)
```
   4.5
 - 1.58
```

(2)
```
   5.65
 - 2.37
```

(6)
```
   7.12
 - 5.4
```

(10)
```
   2.9
 - 0.86
```

(3)
```
   6.32
 - 4.9
```

(7)
```
   4.3
 - 1.62
```

(11)
```
   4.26
 - 1.57
```

(4)
```
   3.04
 - 0.8
```

(8)
```
   5.09
 - 0.2
```

(12)
```
   2.01
 - 0.09
```

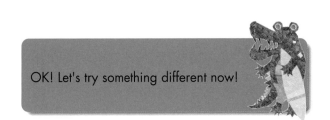

OK! Let's try something different now!

Subtraction of Decimals

Level ★★

Score

/100

Date / /

Name

1 **Subtract.**

4 points per question

Example

```
    1          2          2
  − 0.3      − 0.6      − 1.4
    0.7        1.4        0.6
```

(1)
```
    1
  − 0.4
```

(4)
```
    2
  − 0.7
```

(7)
```
   10
  − 0.6
```

(10)
```
    3
  − 1.4
```

(2)
```
    2
  − 0.4
```

(5)
```
    4
  − 0.3
```

(8)
```
   20
  − 0.3
```

(11)
```
    5
  − 2.7
```

(3)
```
    3
  − 0.8
```

(6)
```
    8
  − 0.6
```

(9)
```
    2
  − 1.2
```

(12)
```
    7
  − 3.8
```

② Subtract.

Example

```
    1          3          3
 − 0.65     − 0.57     − 1.46
 ─────      ─────      ─────
   0.35       2.43       1.54
```

(1)
```
    1
 − 0.6
```

(5)
```
    5
 − 2.83
```

(9)
```
    4
 − 3.27
```

(13)
```
    4
 − 3.03
```

(2)
```
    1
 − 0.63
```

(6)
```
    1
 − 0.07
```

(10)
```
    3
 − 0.27
```

(3)
```
    2
 − 0.54
```

(7)
```
    2
 − 0.04
```

(11)
```
    4
 − 2.08
```

(4)
```
    3
 − 1.27
```

(8)
```
    3
 − 1.06
```

(12)
```
    6
 − 4.95
```

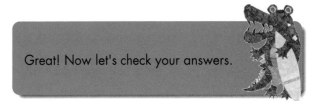

Great! Now let's check your answers.

Subtraction of Decimals

Date / /

Name

Score / 100

1 **Subtract.**

4 points per question

(1) 2.5
   − 1.7

(4) 3.05
   − 0.08

(7) 4
   − 1.72

(10) 1
   − 0.48

(2) 5.27
   − 2.7

(5) 12.4
   − 3.8

(8) 1.02
   − 0.7

(11) 6.2
   − 5.46

(3) 8.63
   − 3.23

(6) 4.5
   − 1.24

(9) 3.94
   − 1.76

(12) 2
   − 0.03

 **Subtract.**

(1) $7.95 - 4.31 =$

(2) $3.6 - 1.8 =$

(3) $6.34 - 2.7 =$

(4) $4.1 - 0.53 =$

(5) $15.9 - 8.9 =$

(6) $2 - 0.8 =$

(7) $3.42 - 1.4 =$

(8) $10.3 - 5.8 =$

(9) $4.53 - 3.72 =$

(10) $3 - 1.42 =$

(11) $7.26 - 3.6 =$

(12) $5.2 - 3.17 =$

(13) $2.05 - 0.09 =$

If you have difficulty solving the problems horizontally, try solving them vertically.

Now let's mix it up a bit!

Three Decimals
◆Addition & Subtraction

22

Level ★★★

Score

Date / /

Name

/100

1 **Calculate.**

4 points per question

(1) 2 + 1.2 + 2.4 = 5.6

(2) 2.3 + 1 + 4.6 = 7.9

(3) 1.8 + 3.2 + 2 = 7.0

(4) 2.4 + 1.6 + 3.5 = 7.5

(5) 1.7 + 4.2 + 2.3 = 9.5

(6) 2.5 + 1.9 + 3.6 = 7.1

(7) 0.6 + 1.9 + 2.4 = 4.9

(8) 3.2 + 0.7 + 2.6 = 6.5

(9) 4.9 + 1.8 + 0.5 = 7.2

(10) 2.3 + 4.2 + 2.7 = 9.2

(11) 2.8 + 3.4 + 5.7 = 11.9

(12) 3.6 + 2.7 + 4.9 = 11.2

② Calculate.

(1) $3.8 + 2 - 1.5 =$

(2) $4.2 + 1.4 - 2.3 =$

(3) $4.3 + 1.2 - 3.9 =$

(4) $2.8 + 0.5 - 0.9 =$

(5) $3.6 + 1.4 - 0.7 =$

(6) $2.5 + 3.6 - 4.7 =$

(7) $2.7 + 1.6 - 3.8 =$

(8) $5.2 - 2 + 1.3 =$

(9) $3.4 - 1.9 + 0.8 =$

(10) $4.3 - 2.6 + 3.4 =$

(11) $6 - 3.2 + 1.7 =$

(12) $5 - 1.3 + 2.6 =$

(13) $4.6 - 2.9 + 3.8 =$

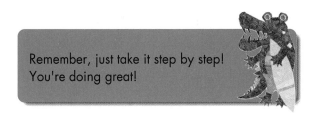

Remember, just take it step by step!
You're doing great!

Three Decimals
◆Addition & Subtraction

23

Level ★★★

Date   /   /

Name

Score   /100

1 Calculate.

4 points per question

(1) $7.4 - 2.1 - 3 =$

(2) $6.2 - 4 - 1.5 =$

(3) $5.8 - 2.4 - 1.3 =$

(4) $7.6 - 1.2 - 3.7 =$

(5) $9.3 - 2.7 - 3.5 =$

(6) $5.4 - 0.9 - 2.3 =$

(7) $7 - 0.4 - 2.7 =$

(8) $8 - 3.2 - 1.8 =$

(9) $9 - 3.7 - 2.6 =$

(10) $6.5 - 3.6 - 0.4 =$

(11) $4.1 - 1.8 - 1.7 =$

(12) $6.2 - 2.8 - 1.5 =$

② Calculate.

(1) $3 + 2.4 + 4.8 =$

(2) $3.4 + 2.7 - 1.8 =$

(3) $8 - 3.4 + 2.6 =$

(4) $5.6 - 1.9 - 2.1 =$

(5) $7 - 2.3 - 3.9 =$

(6) $2.8 + 1.6 + 3.2 =$

(7) $6.2 - 1.7 + 0.6 =$

(8) $4.5 + 2 - 5.7 =$

(9) $2.3 + 0.6 + 1.4 =$

(10) $7.4 - 0.9 - 4.6 =$

(11) $2.6 + 5.6 - 3.8 =$

(12) $4.7 + 2.9 + 1.5 =$

(13) $9 - 2.6 - 4.9 =$

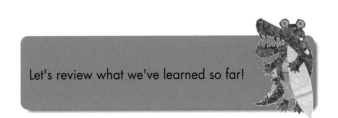

Let's review what we've learned so far!

24 Decimals Review

Level ★★★

Date   /   /

Name

Score   /100

1 Calculate.

5 points per question

(1) 4.7 + 3.9 =

(2) 13.8 + 0.2 =

(3) 8.3 + 5.9 =

(4) 3.92 + 12.7 =

(5) 0.84 + 5.6 =

(6) 0.6 + 2.49 =

(7) 16.9 + 1.54 =

(8) 0.47 + 3.63 =

(9) 2.75 + 1.68 =

(10) 3.62 + 4.39 =

2 Calculate.

5 points per question

(1) 3.1 − 1.5 =

(2) 12.7 − 8 =

(3) 14.6 − 3.6 =

(4) 5.29 − 2.8 =

(5) 3.3 − 1.05 =

(6) 6.2 − 4.57 =

(7) 2.06 − 0.38 =

(8) 4.23 − 2.54 =

(9) 1 − 0.06 =

(10) 3 − 1.72 =

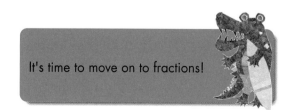

It's time to move on to fractions!

Level ★★

Score

/100

Date 7 /25 /

Name Uthara

1 Rewrite the improper fractions as mixed numbers or whole numbers.

2 points per question

Example $\frac{5}{5} = 1$ $\frac{6}{5} = 1\frac{1}{5}$ $\frac{10}{5} = 2$ $\frac{11}{5} = 2\frac{1}{5}$

(1) $\frac{7}{5} = 1\boxed{\frac{2}{5}}$

(2) $\frac{9}{5} = 1\frac{4}{5}$

(3) $\frac{12}{5} = 2\boxed{\frac{2}{5}}$

(4) $\frac{13}{5} = 2\frac{3}{5}$

(5) $\frac{4}{4} = \boxed{1}\frac{0}{4}$

(6) $\frac{5}{4} = 1\boxed{\frac{1}{4}}$

(7) $\frac{7}{4} = 1\frac{3}{4}$

(8) $\frac{8}{4} = \boxed{2}\frac{0}{4}$

(9) $\frac{9}{4} = 2\frac{1}{4}$

(10) $\frac{11}{4} = 2\frac{3}{4}$

(11) $\frac{6}{6} = 1\frac{0}{6}$

(12) $\frac{7}{6} = 1\frac{1}{6}$

(13) $\frac{12}{6} = 2\frac{0}{6}$

(14) $\frac{13}{6} = 2\frac{1}{6}$

(15) $\frac{9}{7} = 1\frac{2}{7}$

(16) $\frac{13}{7} = 1\frac{6}{7}$

(17) $\frac{15}{7} = 2\frac{1}{7}$

(18) $\frac{10}{9} = 1\frac{1}{9}$

(19) $\frac{14}{9} = 1\frac{5}{9}$

(20) $\frac{18}{9} = 2\frac{0}{9}$

⑤ Uthara 1/2011

(2) Rewrite the improper fractions as mixed numbers or whole numbers.

3 points per question

(1) $\dfrac{8}{5} = 1\dfrac{2}{5}$

(2) $\dfrac{5}{3} = 1\dfrac{2}{3}$

(3) $\dfrac{6}{3} = 2\dfrac{0}{3}$

(4) $\dfrac{7}{3} = 2\dfrac{1}{3}$

(5) $\dfrac{2}{2} = 1\dfrac{0}{2}$

(6) $\dfrac{3}{2} = 1\dfrac{1}{2}$

(7) $\dfrac{5}{2} = 2\dfrac{1}{2}$

(8) $\dfrac{7}{7} = 1\dfrac{0}{7}$

(9) $\dfrac{8}{7} = 1\dfrac{1}{7}$

(10) $\dfrac{16}{7} = 2\dfrac{2}{7}$

(11) $\dfrac{11}{8} = 1\dfrac{3}{8}$

(12) $\dfrac{13}{8} = 1\dfrac{5}{8}$

(13) $\dfrac{16}{8} = 2\dfrac{0}{8}$

(14) $\dfrac{19}{8} = 2\dfrac{3}{8}$

(15) $\dfrac{9}{9} = 1\dfrac{0}{9}$

(16) $\dfrac{13}{9} = 1\dfrac{4}{9}$

(17) $\dfrac{20}{9} = 2\dfrac{2}{9}$

(18) $\dfrac{13}{11} = 1\dfrac{2}{11}$

(19) $\dfrac{17}{11} = 1\dfrac{6}{11}$

(20) $\dfrac{20}{11} = 1\dfrac{9}{11}$

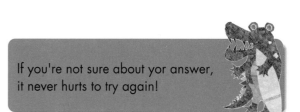

If you're not sure about yor answer, it never hurts to try again!

51

26 Fractions

Level ★★

Date / / Name

Score /100

1 Rewrite the improper fractions as mixed numbers or whole numbers.

2 points per question

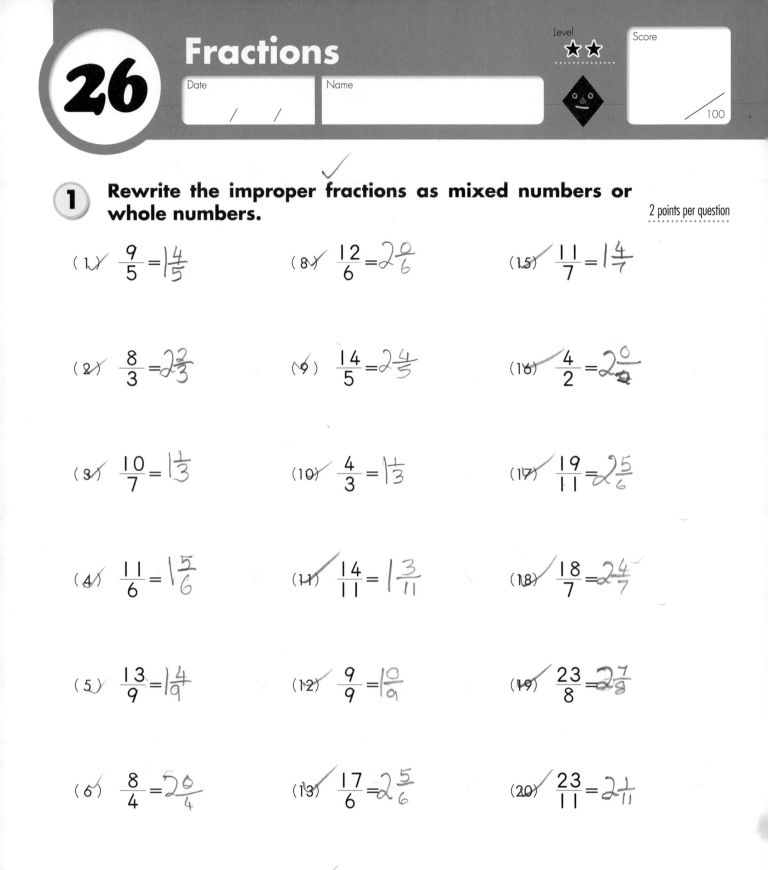

(1) $\frac{9}{5} = 1\frac{4}{5}$

(2) $\frac{8}{3} = 2\frac{2}{3}$

(3) $\frac{10}{7} = 1\frac{7}{3}$

(4) $\frac{11}{6} = 1\frac{5}{6}$

(5) $\frac{13}{9} = 1\frac{4}{9}$

(6) $\frac{8}{4} = 2\frac{0}{4}$

(7) $\frac{13}{7} = 1\frac{6}{7}$

(8) $\frac{12}{6} = 2\frac{0}{6}$

(9) $\frac{14}{5} = 2\frac{4}{5}$

(10) $\frac{4}{3} = 1\frac{1}{3}$

(11) $\frac{14}{11} = 1\frac{3}{11}$

(12) $\frac{9}{9} = 1\frac{0}{9}$

(13) $\frac{17}{6} = 2\frac{5}{6}$

(14) $\frac{10}{9} = 1\frac{1}{9}$

(15) $\frac{11}{7} = 1\frac{4}{7}$

(16) $\frac{4}{2} = 2\frac{0}{2}$

(17) $\frac{19}{11} = 2\frac{5}{6}$

(18) $\frac{18}{7} = 2\frac{4}{7}$

(19) $\frac{23}{8} = 2\frac{7}{8}$

(20) $\frac{23}{11} = 2\frac{1}{11}$

2 Rewrite the improper fractions as mixed numbers or whole numbers.

3 points per question

(1) $\dfrac{5}{3} = 1\dfrac{2}{3}$

(8) $\dfrac{7}{6} = 1\dfrac{1}{6}$

(15) $\dfrac{18}{7} = 2\dfrac{4}{7}$

(2) $\dfrac{15}{7} = 2\dfrac{1}{7}$

(9) $\dfrac{5}{2} = 2\dfrac{4}{2}$

(16) $\dfrac{21}{8} = 2\dfrac{5}{8}$

(3) $\dfrac{12}{6} = 2\dfrac{0}{6}$

(10) $\dfrac{17}{9} = 1\dfrac{8}{9}$

(17) $\dfrac{17}{15} = 1\dfrac{2}{15}$

(4) $\dfrac{11}{9} = 1\dfrac{2}{9}$

(11) $\dfrac{8}{8} = 1\dfrac{0}{8}$

(18) $\dfrac{18}{11} = 1\dfrac{7}{11}$

(5) $\dfrac{11}{5} = 2\dfrac{1}{5}$

(12) $\dfrac{11}{4} = 2\dfrac{3}{4}$

(19) $\dfrac{19}{9} = 2\dfrac{1}{9}$

(6) $\dfrac{4}{4} = 1\dfrac{0}{4}$

(13) $\dfrac{15}{8} = 1\dfrac{7}{8}$

(20) $\dfrac{20}{7} = 2\dfrac{6}{7}$

(7) $\dfrac{17}{11} = 1\dfrac{6}{11}$

(14) $\dfrac{10}{5} = 2\dfrac{0}{5}$

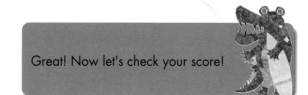

Great! Now let's check your score!

1 Rewrite the improper fractions as mixed numbers or whole numbers.

2 points per question

(1) $\dfrac{6}{5} = 1\dfrac{1}{5}$

(2) $\dfrac{8}{5} = 1$

(3) $\dfrac{10}{5} = 2\dfrac{0}{5}$

(4) $\dfrac{13}{5} = 2\dfrac{3}{5}$

(5) $\dfrac{3}{3} = 1\dfrac{0}{3}$

(6) $\dfrac{8}{3} = 2\dfrac{2}{3}$

(7) $\dfrac{5}{4} = 1\dfrac{1}{4}$

(8) $\dfrac{10}{7} = 1\dfrac{3}{7}$

(9) $\dfrac{15}{7} = 2\dfrac{1}{7}$

(10) $\dfrac{12}{6} = 2\dfrac{0}{6}$

(11) $\dfrac{14}{9} = 1\dfrac{5}{9}$

(12) $\dfrac{20}{9} = 2\dfrac{2}{9}$

2 Rewrite the mixed numbers and whole numbers as improper fractions.

3 points per question

(1) $1 = \dfrac{5}{5}$

(2) $1\dfrac{1}{5} = \dfrac{6}{5}$

(3) $1\dfrac{3}{5} = \dfrac{8}{5}$

(4) $2 = \dfrac{10}{5}$

(5) $2\dfrac{2}{5} = \dfrac{12}{5}$

(6) $1 = \dfrac{3}{3}$

(7) $1\dfrac{2}{3} = \dfrac{5}{3}$

(8) $2\dfrac{1}{3} = \dfrac{7}{3}$

(9) $1 = \dfrac{4}{4}$

(10) $1\dfrac{3}{4} = \dfrac{7}{4}$

(11) $2 = \dfrac{8}{4}$

(12) $2\dfrac{1}{4} = \dfrac{5}{4}$

3 Rewrite the mixed numbers and whole numbers as improper fractions.

2 points per question

(1) $1\frac{4}{5} = \frac{9}{5}$

(8) $1\frac{1}{8} = \frac{9}{8}$

(15) $1\frac{4}{9} = \frac{13}{9}$

(2) $1 = \frac{6}{6}$

(9) $2\frac{1}{5} = \frac{11}{5}$

(16) $2\frac{1}{3} = \frac{7}{3}$

(3) $1\frac{1}{6} = \frac{7}{6}$

(10) $1 = \frac{9}{9}$

(17) $1\frac{6}{7} = \frac{13}{7}$

(4) $1\frac{3}{7} = \frac{10}{7}$

(11) $1\frac{3}{10} = \frac{13}{10}$

(18) $2 = \frac{27}{9}$

(5) $2 = \frac{14}{7}$

(12) $1\frac{2}{11} = \frac{13}{11}$

(19) $2\frac{1}{6} = \frac{13}{6}$

(6) $2\frac{1}{7} = \frac{15}{7}$

(13) $2 = \frac{16}{8}$

(20) $2\frac{1}{9} = \frac{19}{9}$

(7) $2\frac{3}{4} = \frac{11}{4}$

(14) $2\frac{2}{3} = \frac{8}{3}$

OK! Now let's try something new!

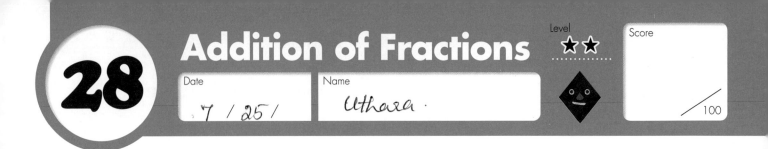

Addition of Fractions

Level ★★

Score /100

Date 7 / 25 /

Name Uthara.

1 Add.

4 points per question

Example

$$\frac{1}{3} + \frac{1}{3} = \frac{2}{3}$$

(1) $\frac{1}{5} + \frac{2}{5} = \frac{3}{5}$

(6) $\frac{2}{7} + \frac{3}{7} = \frac{5}{7}$

(2) $\frac{1}{5} + \frac{3}{5} = \frac{4}{5}$

(7) $\frac{5}{7} + \frac{1}{7} = \frac{6}{7}$

(3) $\frac{2}{5} + \frac{2}{5} = \frac{4}{5}$

(8) $\frac{1}{9} + \frac{3}{9} = \frac{4}{9}$

(4) $\frac{1}{7} + \frac{2}{7} = \frac{3}{7}$

(9) $\frac{1}{9} + \frac{4}{9} = \frac{5}{9}$

(5) $\frac{1}{7} + \frac{3}{7} = \frac{4}{7}$

(10) $\frac{4}{9} + \frac{3}{9} = \frac{7}{9}$

56   © Kumon Publishing Co., Ltd.

 **Add.**

(1) $\dfrac{2}{4} + \dfrac{1}{4} = \dfrac{3}{4}$

(2) $\dfrac{4}{7} + \dfrac{2}{7} = \dfrac{6}{7}$

(3) $\dfrac{2}{8} + \dfrac{5}{8} = \dfrac{7}{8}$

(4) $\dfrac{3}{9} + \dfrac{2}{9} = \dfrac{5}{9}$

(5) $\dfrac{2}{11} + \dfrac{3}{11} = \dfrac{5}{11}$

(6) $\dfrac{7}{13} + \dfrac{4}{13} = \dfrac{11}{13}$

(7) $\dfrac{5}{9} + \dfrac{3}{9} = \dfrac{8}{9}$

(8) $\dfrac{5}{11} + \dfrac{4}{11} = \dfrac{9}{11}$

(9) $\dfrac{3}{10} + \dfrac{4}{10} = \dfrac{7}{10}$

(10) $\dfrac{1}{7} + \dfrac{4}{7} = \dfrac{5}{7}$

(11) $\dfrac{2}{15} + \dfrac{6}{15} = \dfrac{8}{15}$

(12) $\dfrac{6}{15} + \dfrac{7}{15} = \dfrac{13}{15}$

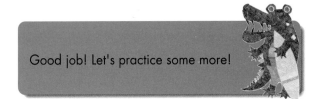

Good job! Let's practice some more!

57

Addition of Fractions

29

Level ★★

Date / /

Name

Score /100

1 ✓ Add.

4 points per question

(1) $\dfrac{2}{5} + \dfrac{1}{5} = \dfrac{3}{5}$

(7) $\dfrac{1}{7} + \dfrac{5}{7} = \dfrac{6}{7}$

(2) $\dfrac{2}{7} + \dfrac{4}{7} = \dfrac{6}{7}$

(8) $\dfrac{6}{11} + \dfrac{2}{11} = \dfrac{8}{11}$

(3) $\dfrac{2}{9} + \dfrac{5}{9} = \dfrac{7}{9}$

(9) $\dfrac{3}{13} + \dfrac{4}{13} = \dfrac{7}{13}$

(4) $\dfrac{3}{11} + \dfrac{4}{11} = \dfrac{7}{11}$

(10) $\dfrac{1}{9} + \dfrac{1}{9} = \dfrac{2}{9}$

(5) $\dfrac{3}{7} + \dfrac{3}{7} = \dfrac{6}{7}$

(11) $\dfrac{4}{15} + \dfrac{9}{15} = \dfrac{13}{15}$

(6) $\dfrac{7}{9} + \dfrac{1}{9} = \dfrac{8}{9}$

(12) $\dfrac{4}{11} + \dfrac{5}{11} = \dfrac{9}{11}$

58 © Kumon Publishing Co., Ltd.

 **Add.**

4 points per question

(1) $\dfrac{3}{5} + \dfrac{1}{5} = \dfrac{4}{5}$

(2) $\dfrac{7}{9} + \dfrac{1}{9} = \dfrac{8}{9}$

(3) $\dfrac{1}{7} + \dfrac{5}{7} = \dfrac{6}{7}$

(4) $\dfrac{6}{11} + \dfrac{4}{11} = \dfrac{10}{11}$

(5) $\dfrac{2}{8} + \dfrac{5}{8} = \dfrac{7}{8}$

(6) $\dfrac{2}{15} + \dfrac{11}{15} = \dfrac{13}{15}$

(7) $\dfrac{10}{17} + \dfrac{6}{17} = \dfrac{16}{17}$

(8) $\dfrac{4}{9} + \dfrac{4}{9} = \dfrac{8}{9}$

(9) $\dfrac{4}{13} + \dfrac{8}{13} = \dfrac{12}{13}$

(10) $\dfrac{7}{15} + \dfrac{6}{15} = \dfrac{13}{15}$

(11) $\dfrac{3}{7} + \dfrac{2}{7} = \dfrac{5}{7}$

(12) $\dfrac{5}{11} + \dfrac{5}{11} = \dfrac{10}{11}$

(13) $\dfrac{9}{17} + \dfrac{6}{17} = \dfrac{15}{17}$

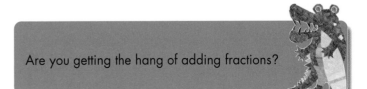

Are you getting the hang of adding fractions?

Addition of Fractions

Level ★ ★

Date / 3 /2011 ①

Name

Score /100

1 Add.

4 points per question

Example

$$\frac{4}{7} + \frac{2}{7} = \frac{6}{7} \qquad \frac{4}{7} + \frac{3}{7} = \frac{7}{7} = 1$$

(1) $\frac{1}{5} + \frac{3}{5} = \frac{4}{5}$

(6) $\frac{3}{7} + \frac{4}{7} = \frac{7}{7}$

(2) $\frac{1}{5} + \frac{4}{5} = \boxed{\frac{5}{5}} = \boxed{3}$

(7) $\frac{4}{9} + \frac{1}{9} = \frac{5}{9}$

(3) $\frac{3}{5} + \frac{2}{5} = \frac{5}{5}$

(8) $\frac{4}{9} + \frac{5}{9} = \frac{9}{9}$

(4) $\frac{2}{7} + \frac{4}{7} = \frac{6}{7}$

(9) $\frac{3}{11} + \frac{5}{11} = \frac{8}{11}$

(5) $\frac{5}{7} + \frac{2}{7} = \frac{7}{7}$

(10) $\frac{8}{11} + \frac{3}{11} = \frac{11}{11}$

2 Add.

(1) $\dfrac{3}{4} + \dfrac{1}{4} =$

(2) $\dfrac{1}{3} + \dfrac{2}{3} =$

(3) $\dfrac{3}{8} + \dfrac{4}{8} =$

(4) $\dfrac{5}{8} + \dfrac{3}{8} =$

(5) $\dfrac{7}{11} + \dfrac{3}{11} =$

(6) $\dfrac{5}{11} + \dfrac{6}{11} =$

(7) $\dfrac{1}{7} + \dfrac{4}{7} =$

(8) $\dfrac{8}{9} + \dfrac{1}{9} =$

(9) $\dfrac{7}{13} + \dfrac{6}{13} =$

(10) $\dfrac{2}{7} + \dfrac{5}{7} =$

(11) $\dfrac{9}{15} + \dfrac{4}{15} =$

(12) $\dfrac{8}{17} + \dfrac{9}{17} =$

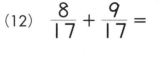

Don't forget to check your answers when you're done.

1 Add.

4 points per question

(1) $\dfrac{1}{5} + \dfrac{2}{5} = \dfrac{3}{5}$

(7) $\dfrac{8}{15} + \dfrac{7}{15} = \dfrac{15}{15}$

(2) $\dfrac{2}{5} + \dfrac{3}{5} = \dfrac{5}{5}$

(8) $\dfrac{4}{15} + \dfrac{7}{15} = \dfrac{11}{15}$

(3) $\dfrac{7}{9} + \dfrac{2}{9} = \dfrac{9}{9}$

(9) $\dfrac{2}{7} + \dfrac{4}{7} = \dfrac{6}{7}$

(4) $\dfrac{5}{9} + \dfrac{2}{9} = \dfrac{7}{9}$

(10) $\dfrac{1}{7} + \dfrac{6}{7} = \dfrac{7}{7}$

(5) $\dfrac{7}{11} + \dfrac{3}{11} = \dfrac{10}{11}$

(11) $\dfrac{7}{17} + \dfrac{6}{17} = \dfrac{13}{17}$

(6) $\dfrac{7}{11} + \dfrac{4}{11} = \dfrac{11}{11}$

(12) $\dfrac{7}{17} + \dfrac{9}{17} = \dfrac{16}{17}$

2/2011 ②

2 Add.

4 points per question

(1) $\dfrac{7}{9} + \dfrac{1}{9} = \dfrac{8}{9}$

(8) $\dfrac{2}{7} + \dfrac{5}{7} = \dfrac{7}{7}$

(2) $\dfrac{2}{11} + \dfrac{9}{11} = \dfrac{11}{11}$

(9) $\dfrac{8}{17} + \dfrac{6}{17} = \dfrac{14}{17}$

(3) $\dfrac{11}{15} + \dfrac{4}{15} = \dfrac{15}{15}$

(10) $\dfrac{4}{5} + \dfrac{1}{5} = \dfrac{5}{5}$

(4) $\dfrac{3}{7} + \dfrac{2}{7} = \dfrac{5}{7}$

(11) $\dfrac{8}{11} + \dfrac{2}{11} = \dfrac{10}{11}$

(5) $\dfrac{7}{13} + \dfrac{4}{13} = \dfrac{11}{13}$

(12) $\dfrac{7}{15} + \dfrac{6}{15} = \dfrac{13}{15}$

(6) $\dfrac{1}{8} + \dfrac{7}{8} = \dfrac{8}{8}$

(13) $\dfrac{8}{17} + \dfrac{9}{17} = \dfrac{17}{17}$

(7) $\dfrac{7}{11} + \dfrac{2}{11} = \dfrac{9}{11}$

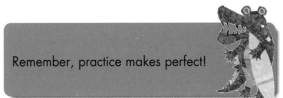

Remember, practice makes perfect!

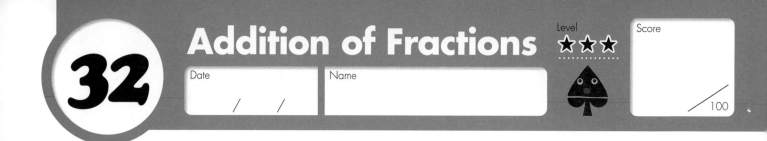

Addition of Fractions

Date   /   /

Name

Score   /100

1 **Add.**

4 points per question

> **Example**
>
> $$\frac{4}{7} + \frac{3}{7} = \frac{7}{7} = 1 \qquad \frac{4}{7} + \frac{5}{7} = \frac{9}{7} = 1\frac{2}{7}$$

(1) $\dfrac{2}{5} + \dfrac{1}{5} = \dfrac{3}{5}$

(2) $\dfrac{2}{5} + \dfrac{3}{5} = \dfrac{5}{5}$

(3) $\dfrac{2}{5} + \dfrac{4}{5} = \dfrac{\boxed{}}{5} = \boxed{}\dfrac{\boxed{}}{5}$

(4) $\dfrac{3}{5} + \dfrac{4}{5} = \dfrac{7}{5}$

(5) $\dfrac{4}{5} + \dfrac{2}{5} = \dfrac{6}{5}$

(6) $\dfrac{5}{7} + \dfrac{2}{7} = \dfrac{7}{7}$

(7) $\dfrac{5}{7} + \dfrac{3}{7} = \dfrac{8}{7}$

(8) $\dfrac{4}{7} + \dfrac{5}{7} = \dfrac{9}{7}$

(9) $\dfrac{5}{9} + \dfrac{4}{9} = \dfrac{9}{9}$

(10) $\dfrac{5}{9} + \dfrac{6}{9} = \dfrac{11}{9}$

 **Add.**

(1) $\dfrac{3}{7} + \dfrac{4}{7} =$

(2) $\dfrac{6}{7} + \dfrac{4}{7} =$

(3) $\dfrac{8}{9} + \dfrac{2}{9} =$

(4) $\dfrac{9}{11} + \dfrac{2}{11} =$

(5) $\dfrac{9}{11} + \dfrac{3}{11} =$

(6) $\dfrac{2}{9} + \dfrac{7}{9} =$

(7) $\dfrac{4}{9} + \dfrac{7}{9} =$

(8) $\dfrac{4}{5} + \dfrac{3}{5} =$

(9) $\dfrac{4}{11} + \dfrac{9}{11} =$

(10) $\dfrac{5}{7} + \dfrac{6}{7} =$

(11) $\dfrac{8}{11} + \dfrac{5}{11} =$

(12) $\dfrac{8}{13} + \dfrac{6}{13} =$

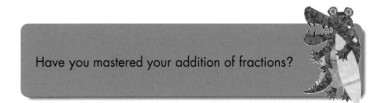

Have you mastered your addition of fractions?

Addition of Fractions

Date   /   /

Name

Score   /100

1 Add.

4 points per question

Example

$$2 + \frac{3}{7} = 2\frac{3}{7}$$

(1) $1 + \frac{3}{4} =$

(6) $\frac{2}{5} + 2 =$

(2) $2 + \frac{5}{7} =$

(7) $\frac{4}{9} + 3 =$

(3) $3 + \frac{3}{8} =$

(8) $\frac{6}{7} + 4 =$

(4) $4 + \frac{5}{9} =$

(9) $\frac{5}{6} + 3 =$

(5) $5 + \frac{7}{11} =$

(10) $\frac{7}{8} + 2 =$

Add.

(1) $\dfrac{2}{7} + \dfrac{4}{7} =$

(2) $\dfrac{4}{5} + \dfrac{3}{5} =$

(3) $\dfrac{3}{11} + \dfrac{4}{11} =$

(4) $\dfrac{1}{9} + \dfrac{7}{9} =$

(5) $\dfrac{2}{3} + \dfrac{2}{3} =$

(6) $3 + \dfrac{7}{8} =$

(7) $\dfrac{5}{9} + \dfrac{4}{9} =$

(8) $\dfrac{6}{11} + \dfrac{8}{11} =$

(9) $\dfrac{4}{7} + \dfrac{3}{7} =$

(10) $\dfrac{3}{4} + 2 =$

(11) $\dfrac{7}{15} + \dfrac{9}{15} =$

(12) $\dfrac{3}{11} + \dfrac{9}{11} =$

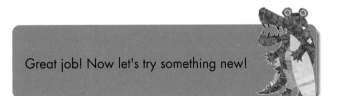

Great job! Now let's try something new!

1 Subtract.

4 points per question

Example

$$\frac{3}{5} - \frac{1}{5} = \frac{2}{5}$$

(1) $\frac{4}{5} - \frac{1}{5} = \frac{3}{5}$

(2) $\frac{4}{5} - \frac{2}{5} = \frac{2}{5}$

(3) $\frac{5}{7} - \frac{2}{7} = \frac{3}{7}$

(4) $\frac{3}{7} - \frac{1}{7} = \frac{2}{7}$

(5) $\frac{6}{7} - \frac{4}{7} = \frac{2}{7}$

(6) $\frac{4}{8} - \frac{1}{8} = \frac{3}{8}$

(7) $\frac{7}{8} - \frac{2}{8} = \frac{5}{8}$

(8) $\frac{5}{9} - \frac{1}{9} = \frac{4}{9}$

(9) $\frac{7}{9} - \frac{5}{9} = \frac{2}{9}$

(10) $\frac{8}{9} - \frac{1}{9} = \frac{7}{9}$

(1) $\dfrac{2}{3} - \dfrac{1}{3} = \dfrac{1}{3}$

(7) $\dfrac{4}{5} - \dfrac{3}{5} = \dfrac{1}{5}$

(2) $\dfrac{6}{7} - \dfrac{2}{7} = \dfrac{4}{7}$

(8) $\dfrac{7}{9} - \dfrac{3}{9} = \dfrac{4}{9}$

(3) $\dfrac{8}{9} - \dfrac{3}{9} = \dfrac{5}{9}$

(9) $\dfrac{8}{11} - \dfrac{2}{11} = 6$

(4) $\dfrac{3}{4} - \dfrac{2}{4} = \dfrac{1}{4}$

(10) $\dfrac{6}{7} - \dfrac{3}{7} = \dfrac{3}{7}$

(5) $\dfrac{5}{7} - \dfrac{4}{7} = \dfrac{1}{7}$

(11) $\dfrac{9}{10} - \dfrac{2}{10} = \dfrac{7}{10}$

(6) $\dfrac{6}{11} - \dfrac{3}{11} =$

(12) $\dfrac{10}{11} - \dfrac{4}{11} = \dfrac{6}{11}$

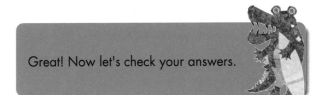

Great! Now let's check your answers.

Date / 1 / 2011 ④

Name Uhara

1 Subtract.

4 points per question

(1) $\dfrac{3}{5} - \dfrac{2}{5} = \dfrac{1}{5}$

(7) $\dfrac{7}{9} - \dfrac{2}{9} = \dfrac{5}{9}$

(2) $\dfrac{4}{7} - \dfrac{1}{7} = \dfrac{3}{7}$

(8) $\dfrac{7}{11} - \dfrac{4}{11} = \dfrac{3}{11}$

(3) $\dfrac{8}{9} - \dfrac{4}{9} = \dfrac{4}{9}$

(9) $\dfrac{9}{13} - \dfrac{4}{13} = \dfrac{5}{13}$

(4) $\dfrac{5}{11} - \dfrac{3}{11} = \dfrac{2}{11}$

(10) $\dfrac{5}{8} - \dfrac{2}{8} = \dfrac{3}{8}$

(5) $\dfrac{6}{7} - \dfrac{5}{7} = \dfrac{1}{7}$

(11) $\dfrac{8}{15} - \dfrac{1}{15} = \dfrac{7}{15}$

(6) $\dfrac{6}{9} - \dfrac{1}{9} = \dfrac{5}{9}$

(12) $\dfrac{9}{11} - \dfrac{3}{11} = \dfrac{6}{11}$

2　Subtract.

4 points per question

(1)　$\dfrac{5}{7} - \dfrac{2}{7} = \dfrac{3}{7}$

(2)　$\dfrac{8}{9} - \dfrac{3}{9} = \dfrac{5}{9}$

(3)　$\dfrac{10}{11} - \dfrac{5}{11} = \dfrac{5}{11}$

(4)　$\dfrac{7}{8} - \dfrac{2}{8} = \dfrac{5}{8}$

(5)　$\dfrac{12}{13} - \dfrac{5}{13} = \dfrac{7}{13}$

(6)　$\dfrac{4}{5} - \dfrac{2}{5} = \dfrac{2}{5}$

(7)　$\dfrac{14}{15} - \dfrac{1}{15} = \dfrac{13}{15}$

(8)　$\dfrac{8}{9} - \dfrac{7}{9} = \dfrac{1}{9}$

(9)　$\dfrac{11}{13} - \dfrac{2}{13} = \dfrac{9}{13}$

(10)　$\dfrac{7}{9} - \dfrac{2}{9} = \dfrac{5}{9}$

(11)　$\dfrac{9}{11} - \dfrac{7}{11} = \dfrac{2}{11}$

(12)　$\dfrac{13}{15} - \dfrac{9}{15} = \dfrac{4}{15}$

(13)　$\dfrac{10}{11} - \dfrac{8}{11} = \dfrac{2}{11}$

If you're not sure about your answer, it never hurts to try again!

Subtraction of Fractions

Level ★★

Date / | / 2011 ①

Name Uthara

Score /100

1 Subtract.

4 points per question

Example

$$\frac{6}{5} - \frac{2}{5} = \frac{4}{5}$$

$\frac{6}{5}$

1

$\frac{2}{5}$

(1) $\frac{6}{5} - \frac{3}{5} = \frac{3}{5}$

(2) $\frac{6}{5} - \frac{4}{5} = \frac{2}{5}$

(3) $\frac{7}{5} - \frac{4}{5} = \frac{3}{5}$

(4) $\frac{8}{7} - \frac{4}{7} = \frac{4}{5}$

(5) $\frac{8}{7} - \frac{5}{7} = \frac{3}{7}$

(6) $\frac{9}{7} - \frac{5}{7} = \frac{4}{7}$

(7) $\frac{9}{7} - \frac{6}{7} = \frac{3}{7}$

(8) $\frac{10}{9} - \frac{5}{9} = \frac{5}{9}$

(9) $\frac{11}{9} - \frac{7}{9} = \frac{4}{9}$

(10) $\frac{12}{11} - \frac{7}{11} = \frac{5}{\pi}$

© Kumon Publishing Co., Ltd.

2 Subtract.

5 points per question

(1) $\dfrac{7}{5} - \dfrac{3}{5} = \dfrac{4}{5}$

(2) $\dfrac{9}{7} - \dfrac{4}{7} = \dfrac{5}{7}$

(3) $\dfrac{4}{3} - \dfrac{2}{3} = \dfrac{2}{3}$

(4) $\dfrac{10}{9} - \dfrac{8}{9} = \dfrac{2}{9}$

(5) $\dfrac{12}{11} - \dfrac{4}{11} = \dfrac{8}{11}$

(6) $\dfrac{10}{7} - \dfrac{5}{7} = \dfrac{5}{7}$

(7) $\dfrac{11}{9} - \dfrac{4}{9} = \dfrac{7}{9}$

(8) $\dfrac{14}{13} - \dfrac{5}{13} = \dfrac{9}{13}$

(9) $\dfrac{13}{11} - \dfrac{6}{11} = \dfrac{7}{11}$

(10) $\dfrac{8}{5} - \dfrac{4}{5} = \dfrac{4}{5}$

(11) $\dfrac{11}{7} - \dfrac{8}{7} = \dfrac{3}{7}$

(12) $\dfrac{14}{11} - \dfrac{5}{11} = \dfrac{9}{11}$

OK! Let's practice some more!

73

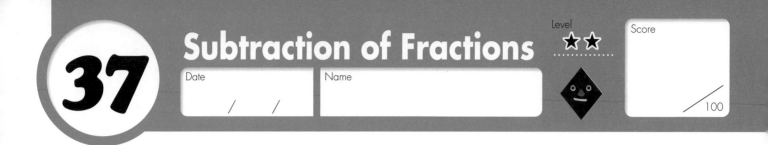

37 Subtraction of Fractions

Level ★★

Date / /

Name

Score /100

1 Write the appropriate number in each box.

5 points per question

(1) $\dfrac{3}{4} + \dfrac{1}{4} = \square$

(4) $\dfrac{3}{5} + \dfrac{\square}{5} = 1$

(2) $\dfrac{3}{4} + \dfrac{\square}{4} = 1$

(5) $\dfrac{3}{7} + \dfrac{\square}{7} = 1$

(3) $\dfrac{4}{5} + \dfrac{\square}{5} = 1$

(6) $\dfrac{7}{9} + \dfrac{\square}{9} = 1$

2 Subtract.

5 points per question

(1) $1 - \dfrac{4}{5} =$

(4) $1 - \dfrac{1}{6} =$

(2) $1 - \dfrac{3}{4} =$

(5) $1 - \dfrac{7}{9} =$

(3) $1 - \dfrac{2}{3} =$

(6) $1 - \dfrac{3}{7} =$

3 Subtract.

Example

$$1 - \frac{2}{5} = \frac{3}{5}$$

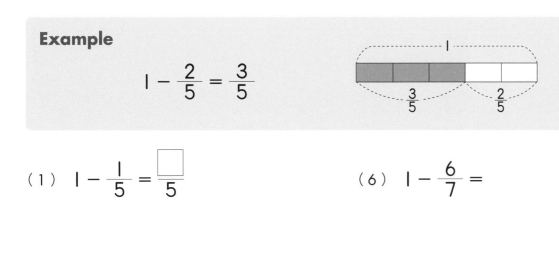

(1) $1 - \dfrac{1}{5} = \dfrac{\boxed{}}{5}$

(2) $1 - \dfrac{1}{3} =$

(3) $1 - \dfrac{4}{5} =$

(4) $1 - \dfrac{3}{8} =$

(5) $1 - \dfrac{3}{10} =$

(6) $1 - \dfrac{6}{7} =$

(7) $1 - \dfrac{5}{9} =$

(8) $1 - \dfrac{5}{11} =$

(9) $1 - \dfrac{2}{7} =$

(10) $1 - \dfrac{8}{11} =$

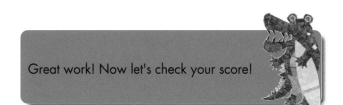

Great work! Now let's check your score!

1 Subtract.

4 points per question

(1) $\dfrac{4}{5} - \dfrac{2}{5} = \dfrac{2}{5}$

(2) $\dfrac{6}{7} - \dfrac{1}{7} = \dfrac{5}{7}$

(3) $\dfrac{7}{9} - \dfrac{3}{9} = \dfrac{4}{9}$

(4) $\dfrac{8}{11} - \dfrac{5}{11} = \dfrac{3}{11}$

(5) $1 - \dfrac{1}{4} =$

(6) $1 - \dfrac{2}{9} =$

(7) $1 - \dfrac{3}{11} =$

(8) $\dfrac{4}{3} - \dfrac{2}{3} = \dfrac{2}{3}$

(9) $\dfrac{8}{7} - \dfrac{6}{7} = \dfrac{2}{7}$

(10) $\dfrac{11}{9} - \dfrac{3}{9} = \dfrac{8}{9}$

(11) $\dfrac{12}{11} - \dfrac{4}{11} = \dfrac{8}{11}$

(12) $\dfrac{14}{13} - \dfrac{8}{13} = \dfrac{6}{13}$

2 **Subtract.**

4 points per question

(1) $\frac{5}{7} - \frac{2}{7} = \frac{3}{7}$

(2) $1 - \frac{5}{8} =$

(3) $\frac{13}{11} - \frac{6}{11} = \frac{7}{11}$

(4) $\frac{11}{9} - \frac{4}{9} = \frac{7}{9}$

(5) $1 - \frac{5}{11} =$

(6) $\frac{3}{4} - \frac{3}{4} = \frac{0}{4}$

(7) $\frac{9}{7} - \frac{3}{7} = \frac{6}{7}$

(8) $1 - \frac{7}{10} =$

(9) $\frac{9}{11} - \frac{4}{11} = \frac{5}{11}$

(10) $\frac{7}{5} - \frac{4}{5} = \frac{3}{5}$

(11) $1 - \frac{8}{9} =$

(12) $\frac{12}{11} - \frac{7}{11} = \frac{5}{11}$

(13) $\frac{8}{9} - \frac{3}{9} = \frac{5}{9}$

Now let's try problems with more than two fractions!

77

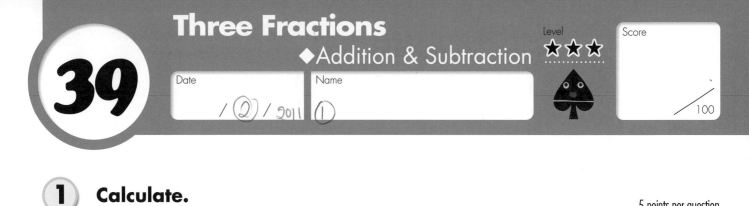

Three Fractions
◆Addition & Subtraction

Level ★★★

Date / ② / 2011

Name ①

Score /100

1 Calculate.

5 points per question

(1) $\dfrac{1}{5} + \dfrac{2}{5} + \dfrac{1}{5} = \dfrac{4}{5}$

(5) $\dfrac{2}{11} + \dfrac{3}{11} + \dfrac{1}{11} = \dfrac{6}{11}$

(2) $\dfrac{2}{7} + \dfrac{1}{7} + \dfrac{3}{7} = \dfrac{6}{7}$

(6) $\dfrac{2}{11} + \dfrac{1}{11} + \dfrac{4}{11} = \dfrac{7}{11}$

(3) $\dfrac{2}{9} + \dfrac{1}{9} + \dfrac{4}{9} = \dfrac{7}{9}$

(7) $\dfrac{2}{15} + \dfrac{1}{15} + \dfrac{4}{15} = \dfrac{7}{15}$

(4) $\dfrac{3}{9} + \dfrac{2}{9} + \dfrac{2}{9} = \dfrac{7}{9}$

(8) $\dfrac{4}{15} + \dfrac{2}{15} + \dfrac{5}{15} = \dfrac{11}{15}$

② Calculate.

6 points per question

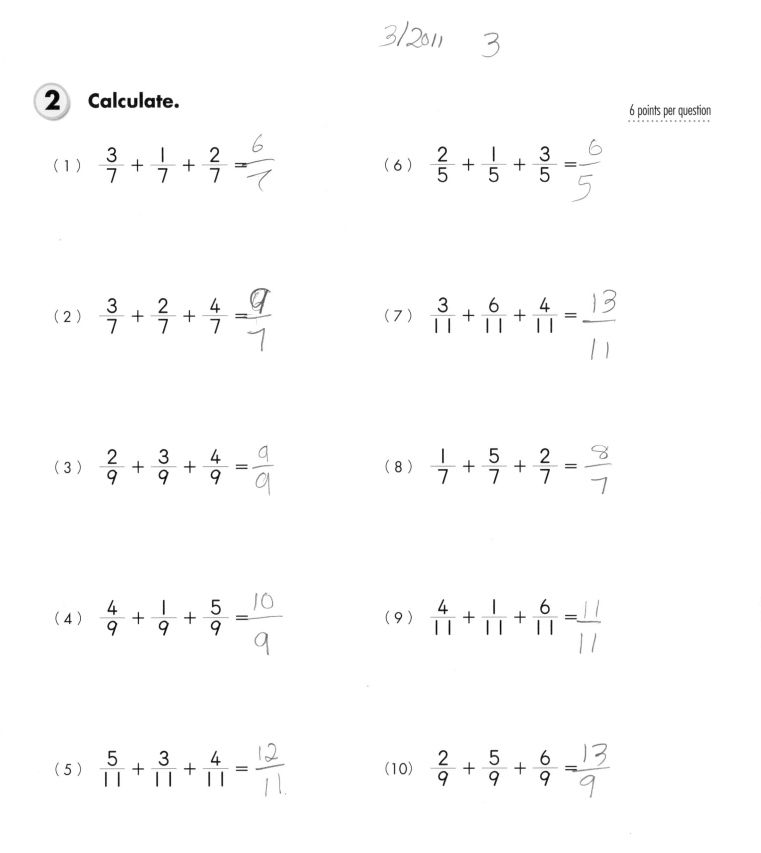

(1) $\dfrac{3}{7} + \dfrac{1}{7} + \dfrac{2}{7} = \dfrac{6}{7}$

(6) $\dfrac{2}{5} + \dfrac{1}{5} + \dfrac{3}{5} = \dfrac{6}{5}$

(2) $\dfrac{3}{7} + \dfrac{2}{7} + \dfrac{4}{7} = \dfrac{9}{7}$

(7) $\dfrac{3}{11} + \dfrac{6}{11} + \dfrac{4}{11} = \dfrac{13}{11}$

(3) $\dfrac{2}{9} + \dfrac{3}{9} + \dfrac{4}{9} = \dfrac{9}{9}$

(8) $\dfrac{1}{7} + \dfrac{5}{7} + \dfrac{2}{7} = \dfrac{8}{7}$

(4) $\dfrac{4}{9} + \dfrac{1}{9} + \dfrac{5}{9} = \dfrac{10}{9}$

(9) $\dfrac{4}{11} + \dfrac{1}{11} + \dfrac{6}{11} = \dfrac{11}{11}$

(5) $\dfrac{5}{11} + \dfrac{3}{11} + \dfrac{4}{11} = \dfrac{12}{11}$

(10) $\dfrac{2}{9} + \dfrac{5}{9} + \dfrac{6}{9} = \dfrac{13}{9}$

Keep up the great work!

79

Three Fractions
◆Addition & Subtraction

40

Level ★★★

Date   /   /

Name

Score   /100

1   Calculate.

5 points per question

(1) $\dfrac{3}{5} + \dfrac{1}{5} - \dfrac{2}{5} =$

(2) $\dfrac{4}{7} + \dfrac{2}{7} - \dfrac{3}{7} =$

(3) $\dfrac{4}{9} + \dfrac{3}{9} - \dfrac{5}{9} =$

(4) $\dfrac{5}{11} + \dfrac{3}{11} - \dfrac{6}{11} =$

(5) $\dfrac{4}{5} - \dfrac{2}{5} + \dfrac{1}{5} =$

(6) $\dfrac{6}{7} - \dfrac{3}{7} + \dfrac{2}{7} =$

(7) $\dfrac{7}{9} - \dfrac{3}{9} + \dfrac{4}{9} =$

(8) $\dfrac{8}{11} - \dfrac{4}{11} + \dfrac{3}{11} =$

 **Calculate.**

(1) $\dfrac{2}{5} + \dfrac{3}{5} - \dfrac{4}{5} =$

(2) $\dfrac{5}{7} - \dfrac{4}{7} + \dfrac{2}{7} =$

(3) $\dfrac{4}{9} + \dfrac{5}{9} - \dfrac{7}{9} =$

(4) $\dfrac{9}{11} - \dfrac{3}{11} + \dfrac{2}{11} =$

(5) $\dfrac{4}{7} + \dfrac{5}{7} - \dfrac{6}{7} =$

(6) $\dfrac{10}{9} - \dfrac{7}{9} + \dfrac{2}{9} =$

(7) $\dfrac{8}{11} + \dfrac{3}{11} - \dfrac{9}{11} =$

(8) $\dfrac{7}{5} - \dfrac{4}{5} + \dfrac{1}{5} =$

(9) $\dfrac{2}{9} + \dfrac{5}{9} - \dfrac{3}{9} =$

(10) $\dfrac{10}{11} - \dfrac{8}{11} + \dfrac{4}{11} =$

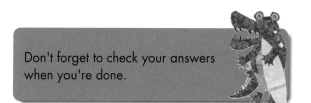

Don't forget to check your answers when you're done.

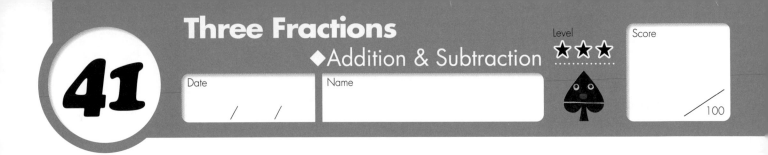

Three Fractions
◆Addition & Subtraction

Level ★★★

Score

/100

Date / /

Name

1 **Calculate.**

5 points per question

(1) $\dfrac{6}{7} - \dfrac{3}{7} - \dfrac{1}{7} =$

(5) $\dfrac{8}{7} - \dfrac{4}{7} - \dfrac{2}{7} =$

(2) $\dfrac{7}{9} - \dfrac{3}{9} - \dfrac{2}{9} =$

(6) $\dfrac{10}{9} - \dfrac{4}{9} - \dfrac{1}{9} =$

(3) $\dfrac{9}{11} - \dfrac{5}{11} - \dfrac{3}{11} =$

(7) $\dfrac{10}{11} - \dfrac{3}{11} - \dfrac{4}{11} =$

(4) $\dfrac{12}{11} - \dfrac{5}{11} - \dfrac{4}{11} =$

(8) $\dfrac{7}{5} - \dfrac{2}{5} - \dfrac{3}{5} =$

 **Calculate.**

6 points per question

(1) $\dfrac{4}{5} + \dfrac{3}{5} - \dfrac{2}{5} =$

(6) $\dfrac{5}{4} - \dfrac{1}{4} - \dfrac{3}{4} =$

(2) $\dfrac{8}{9} - \dfrac{4}{9} + \dfrac{3}{9} =$

(7) $\dfrac{2}{7} + \dfrac{5}{7} - \dfrac{4}{7} =$

(3) $\dfrac{6}{7} - \dfrac{2}{7} - \dfrac{3}{7} =$

(8) $\dfrac{10}{9} - \dfrac{8}{9} + \dfrac{2}{9} =$

(4) $\dfrac{9}{11} - \dfrac{7}{11} + \dfrac{5}{11} =$

(9) $\dfrac{4}{11} + \dfrac{6}{11} - \dfrac{8}{11} =$

(5) $\dfrac{11}{9} - \dfrac{7}{9} - \dfrac{2}{9} =$

(10) $\dfrac{8}{7} - \dfrac{2}{7} - \dfrac{5}{7} =$

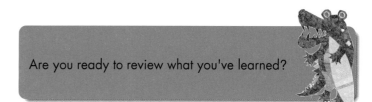

Are you ready to review what you've learned?

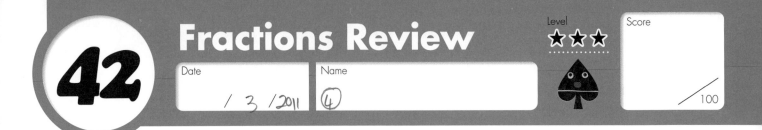

Fractions Review

Date
/ 3 /2011

Name
④

Level
★★★

Score
/100

1 **Calculate.**

4 points per question

(1) $\dfrac{2}{5} + \dfrac{1}{5} = \dfrac{3}{5}$

(2) $\dfrac{2}{7} + \dfrac{3}{7} = \dfrac{5}{7}$

(3) $\dfrac{5}{9} + \dfrac{2}{9} = \dfrac{7}{9}$

(4) $\dfrac{3}{11} + \dfrac{7}{11} = \dfrac{10}{11}$

(5) $\dfrac{4}{7} + \dfrac{3}{7} = \dfrac{7}{7}$

(6) $\dfrac{4}{9} + \dfrac{7}{9} = \dfrac{11}{9}$

(7) $\dfrac{4}{5} + \dfrac{1}{5} = \dfrac{5}{5}$

(8) $\dfrac{5}{7} + \dfrac{3}{7} = \dfrac{8}{7}$

(9) $\dfrac{6}{11} + \dfrac{8}{11} = \dfrac{14}{11}$

(10) $\dfrac{8}{9} + \dfrac{5}{9} = \dfrac{13}{9}$

(11) $\dfrac{7}{8} + 1 = \dfrac{8}{8}$

(12) $2 + \dfrac{3}{7} = \dfrac{5}{7}$

Calculate.

(1) $\dfrac{4}{5} - \dfrac{2}{5} =$

(2) $\dfrac{7}{9} - \dfrac{2}{9} =$

(3) $\dfrac{8}{11} - \dfrac{4}{11} =$

(4) $\dfrac{5}{8} - \dfrac{2}{8} =$

(5) $\dfrac{6}{7} - \dfrac{5}{7} =$

(6) $\dfrac{11}{15} - \dfrac{3}{15} =$

(7) $\dfrac{9}{11} - \dfrac{2}{11} =$

(8) $1 - \dfrac{3}{7} =$

(9) $1 - \dfrac{3}{10} =$

(10) $1 - \dfrac{1}{12} =$

(11) $\dfrac{10}{7} - \dfrac{4}{7} =$

(12) $\dfrac{10}{9} - \dfrac{3}{9} =$

(13) $\dfrac{13}{11} - \dfrac{5}{11} =$

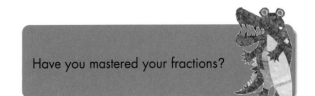

Have you mastered your fractions?

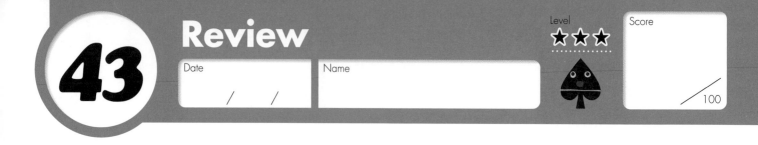

1 Calculate.

4 points per question

(1) $6.5 + 7.8 =$

(2) $9.4 + 0.6 =$

(3) $4.73 + 12.9 =$

(4) $8.2 + 9.84 =$

(5) $2.67 + 0.35 =$

(6) $4.2 - 1.7 =$

(7) $7.06 - 3.5 =$

(8) $5.4 - 3.82 =$

(9) $6.13 - 5.44 =$

(10) $2 - 0.07 =$

2 **Calculate.**

(1) $\dfrac{3}{4} + \dfrac{1}{4} =$

(7) $\dfrac{6}{7} - \dfrac{2}{7} =$

(2) $\dfrac{3}{7} + \dfrac{5}{7} =$

(8) $1 - \dfrac{3}{8} =$

(3) $\dfrac{1}{9} + \dfrac{6}{9} =$

(9) $\dfrac{11}{9} - \dfrac{3}{9} =$

(4) $2 + \dfrac{3}{10} =$

(10) $\dfrac{12}{11} - \dfrac{7}{11} =$

(5) $\dfrac{5}{11} + \dfrac{4}{11} =$

(11) $1 - \dfrac{4}{9} =$

(6) $\dfrac{5}{9} + \dfrac{8}{9} =$

(12) $\dfrac{14}{15} - \dfrac{6}{15} =$

Congratulations! You are ready for **Grade 5 Decimals & Fractions**!

1 Addition & Subtraction Review   pp 2, 3

1
(1) 59	(6) 96	(11) 143	(16) 337
(2) 43	(7) 90	(12) 133	(17) 410
(3) 80	(8) 120	(13) 144	(18) 383
(4) 74	(9) 134	(14) 293	(19) 400
(5) 81	(10) 135	(15) 225	(20) 500

2
(1) 55	(6) 22	(11) 110	(16) 318
(2) 18	(7) 37	(12) 116	(17) 425
(3) 16	(8) 70	(13) 229	(18) 175
(4) 30	(9) 70	(14) 305	(19) 465
(5) 4	(10) 124	(15) 432	(20) 456

2 Decimals   pp 4, 5

1 (Starting from the left)
(1) 0.1, 0.3, 0.5, 0.7, 0.9
(2) 0.2, 0.4, 0.6, 0.8
(3) 0.1, 0.4, 0.7, 0.9
(4) 0.2, 0.3, 0.5, 0.8
(5) 0.3, 0.6, 0.7, 1.1
(6) 0.4, 0.8, 0.9, 1.2

2 (Starting from the left)
(1) 0.1, 0.6, 1.1, 1.5
(2) 0.3, 1.3, 1.6, 1.9
(3) 0.5, 1.2, 1.4, 2.1
(4) 0.7, 1.4, 2.1, 2.2
(5) 0.9, 1.5, 1.9, 2.3
(6) 0.8, 1.3, 1.6, 2.1, 2.4

3 Addition of Decimals   pp 6, 7

1
(1) 1.3	(11) 1.1	(1) 3.1	(11) 1.5
(2) 1.4	(12) 2.1	(2) 3.2	(12) 2.2
(3) 1.6	(13) 2.3	(3) 3.4	(13) 2.4
(4) 1.7	(14) 2.4	(4) 3.7	(14) 4.2
(5) 1.9	(15) 2.7	(5) 3.9	(15) 3.6
(6) 2.1	(16) 2.9	(6) 4.1	(16) 1.8
(7) 2.2	(17) 3.1	(7) 4.3	(17) 4.4
(8) 2.3	(18) 3.3	(8) 4.5	(18) 2.5
(9) 2.5	(19) 3.6	(9) 4.8	(19) 2.7
(10) 2.8	(20) 3.9	(10) 4.9	(20) 4.6

(**2** heads the third/fourth columns above.)

4 Addition of Decimals   pp 8, 9

1
(1) 0.8	(11) 0.9
(2) 0.9	(12) 1
(3) 0.7	(13) 1.1
(4) 0.8	(14) 1
(5) 0.9	(15) 1.1
(6) 1	(16) 1.2
(7) 1.1	(17) 1.4
(8) 1.2	(18) 1.7
(9) 1.3	(19) 1
(10) 1.4	(20) 1.3

2
(1) 0.7	(11) 1.7
(2) 1.7	(12) 2.7
(3) 1.8	(13) 2.8
(4) 1.9	(14) 3.8
(5) 2	(15) 2.9
(6) 2.1	(16) 3.9
(7) 2.2	(17) 5.9
(8) 2.3	(18) 3.6
(9) 2.5	(19) 4.9
(10) 3.5	(20) 5.7

5 Addition of Decimals   pp 10, 11

1
(1) 2.4	(11) 1.6
(2) 3.4	(12) 1.7
(3) 4.4	(13) 1.8
(4) 2.7	(14) 2.3
(5) 3.7	(15) 2.4
(6) 3.5	(16) 2.6
(7) 4.5	(17) 2.7
(8) 3.8	(18) 3.7
(9) 4.8	(19) 3.5
(10) 5.6	(20) 3.9

2
(1) 1.6	(11) 0.9
(2) 4.4	(12) 3
(3) 1.2	(13) 3.9
(4) 1.5	(14) 1.7
(5) 3.8	(15) 1.1
(6) 4.8	(16) 3.8
(7) 3.4	(17) 1
(8) 1.5	(18) 4.2
(9) 2	(19) 4.8
(10) 5.7	(20) 1.4

6 Addition of Decimals   pp 12, 13

1
(1) 3.9	(4) 3.9	(7) 15.6	(10) 5.8
(2) 5.8	(5) 16.8	(8) 12.8	(11) 13.8
(3) 2.8	(6) 15.5	(9) 8.7	(12) 10.8

2
(1) 6.8	(5) 3.4	(9) 13	(13) 14.2
(2) 7.3	(6) 8	(10) 10	
(3) 3.5	(7) 13.6	(11) 5.1	
(4) 4	(8) 10.8	(12) 9.2	

7 Addition of Decimals
pp 14, 15

1
(1) 17.7　(4) 13　(7) 18　(10) 20.5
(2) 18.3　(5) 20.1　(8) 13.2　(11) 22.4
(3) 22.8　(6) 17.7　(9) 23.1　(12) 23.3

2
(1) 4.8　(8) 17
(2) 4.2　(9) 22.6
(3) 7　(10) 16.4
(4) 16.1　(11) 14
(5) 16.8　(12) 10.3
(6) 3.5　(13) 20.2
(7) 10.2

8 Addition of Decimals
pp 16, 17

1
(1) 5.96　(4) 2.87　(7) 7.05　(10) 8.16
(2) 7.78　(5) 6.41　(8) 4.63　(11) 6.28
(3) 3.87　(6) 6.37　(9) 5.03　(12) 8.22

2
(1) 13.76　(5) 19.02　(9) 6.04　(13) 1.03
(2) 21.69　(6) 14.38　(10) 20.27
(3) 12.98　(7) 7.93　(11) 5.47
(4) 18.16　(8) 13.05　(12) 20.15

9 Addition of Decimals
pp 18, 19

1
(1) 5.58　(4) 3.74　(7) 6.07　(10) 9.38
(2) 5.87　(5) 7.33　(8) 5.05　(11) 6.44
(3) 3.75　(6) 4.32　(9) 5.02　(12) 8.16

2
(1) 11.83　(5) 19.03　(9) 16.14　(13) 10.06
(2) 22.86　(6) 7.22　(10) 9.06
(3) 12.88　(7) 10.35　(11) 23.13
(4) 18.44　(8) 8.21　(12) 11.07

10 Addition of Decimals
pp 20, 21

1
(1) 5.77　(4) 5.59　(7) 2.81　(10) 3.9
(2) 7.79　(5) 5.74　(8) 5.6　(11) 7.03
(3) 3.89　(6) 4.94　(9) 4.8　(12) 9

2
(1) 6.89　(5) 6.07　(9) 4.3　(13) 9.03
(2) 8.25　(6) 5.85　(10) 7.11
(3) 4.56　(7) 6.25　(11) 14.88
(4) 3.56　(8) 5.52　(12) 13.95

11 Addition of Decimals
pp 22, 23

1
(1) 5.83　(4) 3.65　(7) 15.08　(10) 4.01
(2) 5.8　(5) 8.21　(8) 10.1　(11) 1.18
(3) 4.38　(6) 11.67　(9) 0.36　(12) 1.04

2
(1) 6.23　(5) 4.44　(9) 0.44　(13) 1.05
(2) 18.52　(6) 9.4　(10) 10
(3) 5.83　(7) 10.32　(11) 1.05
(4) 4.9　(8) 24.38　(12) 10.04

12 Addition of Decimals
pp 24, 25

1
(1) 6.6　(4) 8.26　(7) 6.37　(10) 13.2
(2) 6.13　(5) 18　(8) 8.02　(11) 10.14
(3) 6.84　(6) 9.88　(9) 12.04　(12) 14.15

2
(1) 4.84　(8) 16.3
(2) 7.5　(9) 11.1
(3) 5.48　(10) 10.3
(4) 5.46　(11) 10.35
(5) 18.16　(12) 12.02
(6) 2.9　(13) 5.02
(7) 12.08

13 Subtraction of Decimals
pp 26, 27

1
(1) 0.4　(11) 1.3
(2) 0.3　(12) 1.1
(3) 0.5　(13) 2.1
(4) 0.4　(14) 2.2
(5) 0.6　(15) 2.5
(6) 0.4　(16) 1.3
(7) 0.5　(17) 2.2
(8) 0.3　(18) 3.1
(9) 0.2　(19) 2.4
(10) 0.1　(20) 3.2

2
(1) 1.1　(11) 2.1
(2) 0.7　(12) 1.7
(3) 0.6　(13) 1.6
(4) 1.1　(14) 2.1
(5) 1　(15) 2
(6) 0.9　(16) 1.8
(7) 0.7　(17) 3.2
(8) 0.8　(18) 3
(9) 0.7　(19) 2.7
(10) 0.9　(20) 2.8

14 Subtraction of Decimals

1
(1) 1.6
(2) 1.5
(3) 1.4
(4) 0.4
(5) 0.4
(6) 1.7
(7) 0.7
(8) 0.3
(9) 0.3
(10) 1.6
(11) 2.3
(12) 1.3
(13) 1.2
(14) 2.6
(15) 2.3
(16) 1.3
(17) 1.2
(18) 0.2
(19) 0.3
(20) 0.3

2
(1) 0.5
(2) 2.3
(3) 0.6
(4) 1.5
(5) 2.2
(6) 1
(7) 0.6
(8) 1.8
(9) 1.3
(10) 3
(11) 0.7
(12) 1.2
(13) 2
(14) 0.3
(15) 1.6
(16) 0.2
(17) 2.8
(18) 1.8
(19) 1.2
(20) 0.5

15 Subtraction of Decimals
pp 30, 31

1
(1) 1.5
(2) 2.2
(3) 3.2
(4) 2.1
(5) 12.2
(6) 14.4
(7) 13.4
(8) 10.2
(9) 5.3
(10) 11.2
(11) 5.7
(12) 12.1

2
(1) 1.1
(2) 1
(3) 0.8
(4) 1.8
(5) 2.4
(6) 1.8
(7) 2
(8) 2.9
(9) 0.4
(10) 4.6
(11) 4
(12) 2.9
(13) 1.8

16 Subtraction of Decimals
pp 32, 33

1
(1) 12.2
(2) 11.9
(3) 11.8
(4) 14
(5) 10.8
(6) 9.6
(7) 10.5
(8) 5.7
(9) 11.8
(10) 7.5
(11) 5.8
(12) 3.5

2
(1) 1.6
(2) 3.3
(3) 5.2
(4) 2.8
(5) 14.7
(6) 9.7
(7) 0.6
(8) 9.8
(9) 3
(10) 7.4
(11) 1.8
(12) 6.4
(13) 9.7

17 Subtraction of Decimals
pp 34, 35

1
(1) 4.44
(2) 2.18
(3) 3.12
(4) 4.73
(5) 2.05
(6) 2.68
(7) 4.64
(8) 1.55
(9) 3.07
(10) 1.36
(11) 1.81
(12) 4.63

2
(1) 2.85
(2) 2.05
(3) 0.62
(4) 2.34
(5) 0.65
(6) 5.23
(7) 3.08
(8) 1.77
(9) 0.65
(10) 0.16
(11) 1.02
(12) 3.45
(13) 0.83

18 Subtraction of Decimals
pp 36, 37

1
(1) 3.42
(2) 2.24
(3) 3.44
(4) 2.27
(5) 3.34
(6) 4.3
(7) 4.55
(8) 3.37
(9) 3.66
(10) 1.4
(11) 2.74
(12) 0.8

2
(1) 1.84
(2) 3.6
(3) 3.17
(4) 3.47
(5) 1.77
(6) 1.58
(7) 2.38
(8) 0.86
(9) 2.47
(10) 0.16
(11) 2.53
(12) 3.8
(13) 4.96

19 Subtraction of Decimals
pp 38, 39

1
(1) 2.36
(2) 2.34
(3) 2.36
(4) 1.55
(5) 2.64
(6) 2.62
(7) 4.57
(8) 3.78
(9) 2.77
(10) 6.14
(11) 1.01
(12) 0.85

2
(1) 1.13
(2) 3.28
(3) 1.42
(4) 2.24
(5) 1.78
(6) 1.72
(7) 2.68
(8) 4.89
(9) 0.7
(10) 2.04
(11) 2.69
(12) 1.92
(13) 2.92

20 Subtraction of Decimals
pp 40, 41

1
(1) 0.6
(2) 1.6
(3) 2.2
(4) 1.3
(5) 3.7
(6) 7.4
(7) 9.4
(8) 19.7
(9) 0.8
(10) 1.6
(11) 2.3
(12) 3.2

2
(1) 0.4
(2) 0.37
(3) 1.46
(4) 1.73
(5) 2.17
(6) 0.93
(7) 1.96
(8) 1.94
(9) 0.73
(10) 2.73
(11) 1.92
(12) 1.05
(13) 0.97

21 Subtraction of Decimals pp 42,43

1 (1) 0.8 (4) 2.97 (7) 2.28 (10) 0.52
(2) 2.57 (5) 8.6 (8) 0.32 (11) 0.74
(3) 5.4 (6) 3.26 (9) 2.18 (12) 1.97

2 (1) 3.64 (8) 4.5
(2) 1.8 (9) 0.81
(3) 3.64 (10) 1.58
(4) 3.57 (11) 3.66
(5) 7 (12) 2.03
(6) 1.2 (13) 1.96
(7) 2.02

22 Three Decimals ◆Addition & Subtraction pp 44,45

1 (1) 5.6 (7) 4.9
(2) 7.9 (8) 6.5
(3) 7 (9) 7.2
(4) 7.5 (10) 9.2
(5) 8.2 (11) 11.9
(6) 8 (12) 11.2

2 (1) 4.3 (8) 4.5
(2) 3.3 (9) 2.3
(3) 1.6 (10) 5.1
(4) 2.4 (11) 4.5
(5) 4.3 (12) 6.3
(6) 1.4 (13) 5.5
(7) 0.5

23 Three Decimals ◆Addition & Subtraction pp 46,47

1 (1) 2.3 (7) 3.9
(2) 0.7 (8) 3
(3) 2.1 (9) 2.7
(4) 2.7 (10) 2.5
(5) 3.1 (11) 0.6
(6) 2.2 (12) 1.9

2 (1) 10.2 (8) 0.8
(2) 4.3 (9) 4.3
(3) 7.2 (10) 1.9
(4) 1.6 (11) 4.4
(5) 0.8 (12) 9.1
(6) 7.6 (13) 1.5
(7) 5.1

24 Decimals Review pp 48,49

1 (1) 8.6 (6) 3.09
(2) 14 (7) 18.44
(3) 14.2 (8) 4.1
(4) 16.62 (9) 4.43
(5) 6.44 (10) 8.01

2 (1) 1.6 (6) 1.63
(2) 4.7 (7) 1.68
(3) 11 (8) 1.69
(4) 2.49 (9) 0.94
(5) 2.25 (10) 1.28

25 Fractions pp 50,51

1 (1) $1\frac{2}{5}$ (8) 2 (15) $1\frac{2}{7}$
(2) $1\frac{4}{5}$ (9) $2\frac{1}{4}$ (16) $1\frac{6}{7}$
(3) $2\frac{2}{5}$ (10) $2\frac{3}{4}$ (17) $2\frac{1}{7}$
(4) $2\frac{3}{5}$ (11) 1 (18) $1\frac{1}{9}$
(5) 1 (12) $1\frac{1}{6}$ (19) $1\frac{5}{9}$
(6) $1\frac{1}{4}$ (13) 2 (20) 2
(7) $1\frac{3}{4}$ (14) $2\frac{1}{6}$

2 (1) $1\frac{3}{5}$ (8) 1 (15) 1
(2) $1\frac{2}{3}$ (9) $1\frac{1}{7}$ (16) $1\frac{4}{9}$
(3) 2 (10) $2\frac{2}{7}$ (17) $2\frac{2}{9}$
(4) $2\frac{1}{3}$ (11) $1\frac{3}{8}$ (18) $1\frac{2}{11}$
(5) 1 (12) $1\frac{5}{8}$ (19) $1\frac{6}{11}$
(6) $1\frac{1}{2}$ (13) 2 (20) $1\frac{9}{11}$
(7) $2\frac{1}{2}$ (14) $2\frac{3}{8}$

26 Fractions

1
(1) $1\frac{4}{5}$ (8) 2 (15) $1\frac{4}{7}$
(2) $2\frac{2}{3}$ (9) $2\frac{4}{5}$ (16) 2
(3) $1\frac{3}{7}$ (10) $1\frac{1}{3}$ (17) $1\frac{8}{11}$
(4) $1\frac{5}{6}$ (11) $1\frac{3}{11}$ (18) $2\frac{4}{7}$
(5) $1\frac{4}{9}$ (12) 1 (19) $2\frac{7}{8}$
(6) 2 (13) $2\frac{5}{6}$ (20) $2\frac{1}{11}$
(7) $1\frac{6}{7}$ (14) $1\frac{1}{9}$

2
(1) $1\frac{2}{3}$ (8) $1\frac{1}{6}$ (15) $2\frac{4}{7}$
(2) $2\frac{1}{7}$ (9) $2\frac{1}{2}$ (16) $2\frac{5}{8}$
(3) 2 (10) $1\frac{8}{9}$ (17) $1\frac{2}{15}$
(4) $1\frac{2}{9}$ (11) 1 (18) $1\frac{7}{11}$
(5) $2\frac{1}{5}$ (12) $2\frac{3}{4}$ (19) $2\frac{1}{9}$
(6) 1 (13) $1\frac{7}{8}$ (20) $2\frac{6}{7}$
(7) $1\frac{6}{11}$ (14) 2

27 Fractions
pp 54,55

1
(1) $1\frac{1}{5}$ (5) 1 (9) $2\frac{1}{7}$
(2) $1\frac{3}{5}$ (6) $2\frac{2}{3}$ (10) 2
(3) 2 (7) $1\frac{1}{4}$ (11) $1\frac{5}{9}$
(4) $2\frac{3}{5}$ (8) $1\frac{3}{7}$ (12) $2\frac{2}{9}$

2
(1) $\boxed{\frac{5}{5}}$ (5) $\frac{12}{5}$ (9) $\boxed{\frac{4}{4}}$
(2) $\boxed{\frac{6}{5}}$ (6) $\boxed{\frac{3}{3}}$ (10) $\frac{7}{4}$
(3) $\frac{8}{5}$ (7) $\frac{5}{3}$ (11) $\boxed{\frac{8}{4}}$
(4) $\boxed{\frac{10}{5}}$ (8) $\frac{7}{3}$ (12) $\frac{9}{4}$

3
(1) $\frac{9}{5}$ (8) $\frac{9}{8}$ (15) $\frac{13}{9}$
(2) $\boxed{\frac{6}{6}}$ (9) $\frac{11}{5}$ (16) $\frac{7}{3}$
(3) $\frac{7}{6}$ (10) $\boxed{\frac{9}{9}}$ (17) $\frac{13}{7}$
(4) $\frac{10}{7}$ (11) $\frac{13}{10}$ (18) $\boxed{\frac{18}{9}}$
(5) $\boxed{\frac{14}{7}}$ (12) $\frac{13}{11}$ (19) $\frac{13}{6}$
(6) $\frac{15}{7}$ (13) $\boxed{\frac{16}{8}}$ (20) $\frac{19}{9}$
(7) $\frac{11}{4}$ (14) $\frac{8}{3}$

28 Addition of Fractions
pp 56,57

1
(1) $\boxed{\frac{3}{5}}$ (6) $\frac{5}{7}$
(2) $\frac{4}{5}$ (7) $\frac{6}{7}$
(3) $\frac{4}{5}$ (8) $\frac{4}{9}$
(4) $\boxed{\frac{3}{7}}$ (9) $\frac{5}{9}$
(5) $\frac{4}{7}$ (10) $\frac{7}{9}$

2
(1) $\frac{3}{4}$ (7) $\frac{8}{9}$
(2) $\frac{6}{7}$ (8) $\frac{9}{11}$
(3) $\frac{7}{8}$ (9) $\frac{7}{10}$
(4) $\frac{5}{9}$ (10) $\frac{5}{7}$
(5) $\frac{5}{11}$ (11) $\frac{8}{15}$
(6) $\frac{11}{13}$ (12) $\frac{13}{15}$

29 Addition of Fractions
pp 58,59

1
(1) $\frac{3}{5}$ (7) $\frac{6}{7}$
(2) $\frac{6}{7}$ (8) $\frac{8}{11}$
(3) $\frac{7}{9}$ (9) $\frac{7}{13}$
(4) $\frac{7}{11}$ (10) $\frac{2}{9}$
(5) $\frac{6}{7}$ (11) $\frac{13}{15}$
(6) $\frac{8}{9}$ (12) $\frac{9}{11}$

2
(1) $\frac{4}{5}$ (8) $\frac{8}{9}$
(2) $\frac{8}{9}$ (9) $\frac{12}{13}$
(3) $\frac{6}{7}$ (10) $\frac{13}{15}$
(4) $\frac{10}{11}$ (11) $\frac{5}{7}$
(5) $\frac{7}{8}$ (12) $\frac{10}{11}$
(6) $\frac{13}{15}$ (13) $\frac{15}{17}$
(7) $\frac{16}{17}$

30 Addition of Fractions

1
(1) $\dfrac{4}{5}$

(2) $\dfrac{1}{5} + \dfrac{4}{5} = \dfrac{\boxed{5}}{5} = \boxed{1}$

(3) 1

(4) $\dfrac{6}{7}$

(5) $\dfrac{5}{7} + \dfrac{2}{7} = \dfrac{7}{7} = 1$

(6) 1

(7) $\dfrac{5}{9}$

(8) $\dfrac{4}{9} + \dfrac{5}{9} = \dfrac{9}{9} = 1$

(9) $\dfrac{8}{11}$

(10) $\dfrac{8}{11} + \dfrac{3}{11} = \dfrac{11}{11} = 1$

2
(1) 1

(2) 1

(3) $\dfrac{7}{8}$

(4) 1

(5) $\dfrac{10}{11}$

(6) 1

(7) $\dfrac{5}{7}$

(8) 1

(9) 1

(10) 1

(11) $\dfrac{13}{15}$

(12) 1

31 Addition of Fractions

1
(1) $\dfrac{3}{5}$

(2) 1

(3) 1

(4) $\dfrac{7}{9}$

(5) $\dfrac{10}{11}$

(6) 1

(7) 1

(8) $\dfrac{11}{15}$

(9) $\dfrac{6}{7}$

(10) 1

(11) $\dfrac{13}{17}$

(12) $\dfrac{16}{17}$

2
(1) $\dfrac{8}{9}$

(2) 1

(3) 1

(4) $\dfrac{5}{7}$

(5) $\dfrac{11}{13}$

(6) 1

(7) $\dfrac{9}{11}$

(8) 1

(9) $\dfrac{14}{17}$

(10) 1

(11) $\dfrac{10}{11}$

(12) $\dfrac{13}{15}$

(13) 1

32 Addition of Fractions

1
(1) $\dfrac{3}{5}$

(2) 1

(3) $\dfrac{2}{5} + \dfrac{4}{5} = \dfrac{\boxed{6}}{5} = \boxed{1}\dfrac{\boxed{1}}{5}$

(4) $\dfrac{3}{5} + \dfrac{4}{5} = \dfrac{7}{5} = 1\dfrac{2}{5}$

(5) $1\dfrac{1}{5}$

(6) 1

(7) $\dfrac{5}{7} + \dfrac{3}{7} = \dfrac{8}{7} = 1\dfrac{1}{7}$

(8) $1\dfrac{2}{7}$

(9) 1

(10) $\dfrac{5}{9} + \dfrac{6}{9} = \dfrac{11}{9} = 1\dfrac{2}{9}$

2
(1) 1

(2) $1\dfrac{3}{7}$

(3) $1\dfrac{1}{9}$

(4) 1

(5) $\dfrac{9}{11} + \dfrac{3}{11} = \dfrac{12}{11} = 1\dfrac{1}{11}$

(6) 1

(7) $1\dfrac{2}{9}$

(8) $1\dfrac{2}{5}$

(9) $1\dfrac{2}{11}$

(10) $1\dfrac{4}{7}$

(11) $1\dfrac{2}{11}$

(12) $\dfrac{8}{13} + \dfrac{6}{13} = \dfrac{14}{13} = 1\dfrac{1}{13}$

33 Addition of Fractions

1
(1) $1\dfrac{3}{4}$

(2) $2\dfrac{5}{7}$

(3) $3\dfrac{3}{8}$

(4) $4\dfrac{5}{9}$

(5) $5\dfrac{7}{11}$

(6) $2\dfrac{2}{5}$

(7) $3\dfrac{4}{9}$

(8) $4\dfrac{6}{7}$

(9) $3\dfrac{5}{6}$

(10) $2\dfrac{7}{8}$

2
(1) $\dfrac{6}{7}$

(2) $1\dfrac{2}{5}$

(3) $\dfrac{7}{11}$

(4) $\dfrac{8}{9}$

(5) $1\dfrac{1}{3}$

(6) $3\dfrac{7}{8}$

(7) 1

(8) $1\dfrac{3}{11}$

(9) 1

(10) $2\dfrac{3}{4}$

(11) $1\dfrac{1}{15}$

(12) $1\dfrac{1}{11}$

34 Subtraction of Fractions
pp 68,69

1
(1) $\dfrac{3}{5}$ (6) $\dfrac{3}{8}$

(2) $\dfrac{2}{5}$ (7) $\dfrac{5}{8}$

(3) $\dfrac{3}{7}$ (8) $\dfrac{4}{9}$

(4) $\dfrac{2}{7}$ (9) $\dfrac{2}{9}$

(5) $\dfrac{2}{7}$ (10) $\dfrac{7}{9}$

2
(1) $\dfrac{1}{3}$ (7) $\dfrac{1}{5}$

(2) $\dfrac{4}{7}$ (8) $\dfrac{4}{9}$

(3) $\dfrac{5}{9}$ (9) $\dfrac{6}{11}$

(4) $\dfrac{1}{4}$ (10) $\dfrac{3}{7}$

(5) $\dfrac{1}{7}$ (11) $\dfrac{7}{10}$

(6) $\dfrac{3}{11}$ (12) $\dfrac{6}{11}$

35 Subtraction of Fractions
pp 70,71

1
(1) $\dfrac{1}{5}$ (7) $\dfrac{5}{9}$

(2) $\dfrac{3}{7}$ (8) $\dfrac{3}{11}$

(3) $\dfrac{4}{9}$ (9) $\dfrac{5}{13}$

(4) $\dfrac{2}{11}$ (10) $\dfrac{3}{8}$

(5) $\dfrac{1}{7}$ (11) $\dfrac{7}{15}$

(6) $\dfrac{5}{9}$ (12) $\dfrac{6}{11}$

2
(1) $\dfrac{3}{7}$ (8) $\dfrac{1}{9}$

(2) $\dfrac{5}{9}$ (9) $\dfrac{9}{13}$

(3) $\dfrac{5}{11}$ (10) $\dfrac{5}{9}$

(4) $\dfrac{5}{8}$ (11) $\dfrac{2}{11}$

(5) $\dfrac{7}{13}$ (12) $\dfrac{4}{15}$

(6) $\dfrac{2}{5}$ (13) $\dfrac{2}{11}$

(7) $\dfrac{13}{15}$

36 Subtraction of Fractions
pp 72,73

1
(1) $\dfrac{3}{5}$ (6) $\dfrac{4}{7}$

(2) $\dfrac{2}{5}$ (7) $\dfrac{3}{7}$

(3) $\dfrac{3}{5}$ (8) $\dfrac{5}{9}$

(4) $\dfrac{4}{7}$ (9) $\dfrac{4}{9}$

(5) $\dfrac{3}{7}$ (10) $\dfrac{5}{11}$

2
(1) $\dfrac{4}{5}$ (7) $\dfrac{7}{9}$

(2) $\dfrac{5}{7}$ (8) $\dfrac{9}{13}$

(3) $\dfrac{2}{3}$ (9) $\dfrac{7}{11}$

(4) $\dfrac{2}{9}$ (10) $\dfrac{4}{5}$

(5) $\dfrac{8}{11}$ (11) $\dfrac{3}{7}$

(6) $\dfrac{5}{7}$ (12) $\dfrac{9}{11}$

37 Subtraction of Fractions
pp 74,75

1
(1) $\dfrac{3}{4} + \dfrac{1}{4} = \boxed{1}$ (4) $\dfrac{3}{5} + \dfrac{\boxed{2}}{5} = 1$

(2) $\dfrac{3}{4} + \dfrac{\boxed{1}}{4} = 1$ (5) $\dfrac{3}{7} + \dfrac{\boxed{4}}{7} = 1$

(3) $\dfrac{4}{5} + \dfrac{\boxed{1}}{5} = 1$ (6) $\dfrac{7}{9} + \dfrac{\boxed{2}}{9} = 1$

2
(1) $\dfrac{1}{5}$ (4) $\dfrac{5}{6}$

(2) $\dfrac{1}{4}$ (5) $\dfrac{2}{9}$

(3) $\dfrac{1}{3}$ (6) $\dfrac{4}{7}$

3
(1) $\dfrac{\boxed{4}}{5}$ (6) $\dfrac{1}{7}$

(2) $\dfrac{2}{3}$ (7) $\dfrac{4}{9}$

(3) $\dfrac{1}{5}$ (8) $\dfrac{6}{11}$

(4) $\dfrac{5}{8}$ (9) $\dfrac{5}{7}$

(5) $\dfrac{7}{10}$ (10) $\dfrac{3}{11}$

38 Subtraction of Fractions
pp 76,77

1
(1) $\dfrac{2}{5}$ (7) $\dfrac{8}{11}$

(2) $\dfrac{5}{7}$ (8) $\dfrac{2}{3}$

(3) $\dfrac{4}{9}$ (9) $\dfrac{2}{7}$

(4) $\dfrac{3}{11}$ (10) $\dfrac{8}{9}$

(5) $\dfrac{3}{4}$ (11) $\dfrac{8}{11}$

(6) $\dfrac{7}{9}$ (12) $\dfrac{6}{13}$

2
(1) $\dfrac{3}{7}$ (8) $\dfrac{3}{10}$

(2) $\dfrac{3}{8}$ (9) $\dfrac{5}{11}$

(3) $\dfrac{7}{11}$ (10) $\dfrac{3}{5}$

(4) $\dfrac{7}{9}$ (11) $\dfrac{1}{9}$

(5) $\dfrac{6}{11}$ (12) $\dfrac{5}{11}$

(6) 0 (13) $\dfrac{5}{9}$

(7) $\dfrac{6}{7}$

39 Three Fractions ◆Addition & Subtraction pp 78,79

1
(1) $\frac{4}{5}$ (5) $\frac{6}{11}$

(2) $\frac{6}{7}$ (6) $\frac{7}{11}$

(3) $\frac{7}{9}$ (7) $\frac{7}{15}$

(4) $\frac{7}{9}$ (8) $\frac{11}{15}$

2
(1) $\frac{3}{7}+\frac{1}{7}+\frac{2}{7}=\frac{6}{7}$

(2) $\frac{3}{7}+\frac{2}{7}+\frac{4}{7}=\frac{9}{7}=1\frac{2}{7}$

(3) $\frac{2}{9}+\frac{3}{9}+\frac{4}{9}=\frac{9}{9}=1$

(4) $\frac{4}{9}+\frac{1}{9}+\frac{5}{9}=\frac{10}{9}=1\frac{1}{9}$

(5) $\frac{5}{11}+\frac{3}{11}+\frac{4}{11}=\frac{12}{11}=1\frac{1}{11}$

(6) $\frac{2}{5}+\frac{1}{5}+\frac{3}{5}=\frac{6}{5}=1\frac{1}{5}$

(7) $1\frac{2}{11}$

(8) $1\frac{1}{7}$

(9) 1

(10) $1\frac{4}{9}$

40 Three Fractions ◆Addition & Subtraction pp 80,81

1
(1) $\frac{2}{5}$ (5) $\frac{3}{5}$

(2) $\frac{3}{7}$ (6) $\frac{5}{7}$

(3) $\frac{2}{9}$ (7) $\frac{8}{9}$

(4) $\frac{2}{11}$ (8) $\frac{7}{11}$

2
(1) $\frac{1}{5}$ (6) $\frac{5}{9}$

(2) $\frac{3}{7}$ (7) $\frac{2}{11}$

(3) $\frac{2}{9}$ (8) $\frac{4}{5}$

(4) $\frac{8}{11}$ (9) $\frac{4}{9}$

(5) $\frac{3}{7}$ (10) $\frac{6}{11}$

41 Three Fractions ◆Addition & Subtraction pp 82,83

1
(1) $\frac{2}{7}$ (5) $\frac{2}{7}$

(2) $\frac{2}{9}$ (6) $\frac{5}{9}$

(3) $\frac{1}{11}$ (7) $\frac{3}{11}$

(4) $\frac{3}{11}$ (8) $\frac{2}{5}$

2
(1) 1 (6) $\frac{1}{4}$

(2) $\frac{7}{9}$ (7) $\frac{3}{7}$

(3) $\frac{1}{7}$ (8) $\frac{4}{9}$

(4) $\frac{7}{11}$ (9) $\frac{2}{11}$

(5) $\frac{2}{9}$ (10) $\frac{1}{7}$

42 Fractions Review pp 84,85

1
(1) $\frac{3}{5}$ (7) 1

(2) $\frac{5}{7}$ (8) $1\frac{1}{7}$

(3) $\frac{7}{9}$ (9) $1\frac{3}{11}$

(4) $\frac{10}{11}$ (10) $1\frac{4}{9}$

(5) 1 (11) $1\frac{7}{8}$

(6) $1\frac{2}{9}$ (12) $2\frac{3}{7}$

2
(1) $\frac{2}{5}$ (8) $\frac{4}{7}$

(2) $\frac{5}{9}$ (9) $\frac{7}{10}$

(3) $\frac{4}{11}$ (10) $\frac{11}{12}$

(4) $\frac{3}{8}$ (11) $\frac{6}{7}$

(5) $\frac{1}{7}$ (12) $\frac{7}{9}$

(6) $\frac{8}{15}$ (13) $\frac{8}{11}$

(7) $\frac{7}{11}$

1
(1) 14.3   (6) 2.5
(2) 10   (7) 3.56
(3) 17.63   (8) 1.58
(4) 18.04   (9) 0.69
(5) 3.02   (10) 1.93

2
(1) 1   (7) $\frac{4}{7}$

(2) $1\frac{1}{7}$ (8) $\frac{5}{8}$

(3) $\frac{7}{9}$ (9) $\frac{8}{9}$

(4) $2\frac{3}{10}$ (10) $\frac{5}{11}$

(5) $\frac{9}{11}$ (11) $\frac{5}{9}$

(6) $1\frac{4}{9}$ (12) $\frac{8}{15}$

Advice

If you made many mistakes in **1**, start reviewing on page 6.

If you made many mistakes in **2**, start reviewing on page 50.